# THE LIBRARY
# OF LACTANTIUS

# THE LIBRARY
# OF LACTANTIUS

BY

R. M. OGILVIE

CLARENDON PRESS · OXFORD
1978

*Oxford University Press, Walton Street, Oxford* OX2 6DP

OXFORD   LONDON   GLASGOW   NEW YORK
TORONTO   MELBOURNE   WELLINGTON   CAPE TOWN
IBADAN   NAIROBI   DAR ES SALAAM
KUALA LUMPUR   SINGAPORE   JAKARTA   HONG KONG   TOKYO
DELHI   BOMBAY   CALCUTTA   MADRAS   KARACHI

**British Library Cataloguing in Publication Data**

Ogilvie, Robert Maxwell
  The library of Lactantius.
  1. Lactantius, Lucius Caecilius Firmianus – Books and reading
  I. Title
  028'9          BR1720.LZ          78-40087
  ISBN 0-19-826645-6

*Printed in Great Britain by
William Clowes & Sons Limited, London, Beccles and Colchester*

# Preface

LACTANTIUS has always commanded respect and admiration
for his Latinity, but it is only in recent years that his message
has seemed relevant once again. Lactantius lived in an age of
bureaucracy, inflation, and narrow-minded ideology, when
civilized men had lost confidence in their world and when
powerful external forces were threatening the very existence
and freedom of the Roman way of life. At such a time of crisis
Lactantius, with all the resources of the classical inheritance
behind him, turned to the God of the Christians. This makes
his writing all the more significant for us today.

He was not a great thinker but he is very representative of
his times, and his ideas deserve much more attention than they
have so far received. My immediate purpose, however, is to
give a detailed analysis of his literary background—what he
had actually read—but I hope later to examine the arguments
which he advances in defence of his Christianity. My chief debt
is to the Dean of Christ Church, the Very Revd. Henry Chad-
wick, who has encouraged my studies over many years. I am
also deeply grateful to my colleagues at St. Andrews, especially
Professor I. G. Kidd, Mr. R. P. H. Green, Mr. P. G. Wood-
ward, and Dr. A. S. Gratwick, and other friends, such as
Professor Hugh Lloyd-Jones and Professor M. L. West who
have patiently answered my queries, and especially M. P.
Monat for his help and advice on Lactantius' Bible. I also owe
much to Mrs. Hamilton-Miller, Miss Cleghorn, and Mrs.
Dick for typing illegible drafts. That the Clarendon Press
should have the vision to publish a work of this kind in these
times does more than anything else to sustain one's faith in the
humane values.

In dedicating this book to the Worshipful Company of
Skinners, with their permission, I should like to pay tribute to
the honour that they did me in inviting me to be Headmaster
of Tonbridge School, whose virtues Lactantius would have
recognized.

Finally I would thank James Corin for his interest and inspiration over the years.

*Errachd*                                                   R. M. OGILVIE

# Contents

# Abbreviations

I HAVE used standard abbreviations for books and periodicals. The following are the most commonly cited collections of fragments:

Aristotle       *Fragmenta selecta* . . . recognovit W. D. Ross (Oxford, 1955)

Callimachus     Ed. R. Pfeiffer (Oxford, 1948–53)

Chrysippus      H. F. von Arnim, *Stoicorum Veterum Fragmenta* (Leipzig, 1903–5)

Cicero          *M. Tullii Ciceronis scripta omnia*: rec. R. Klotz (Pars IV: Leipzig, 1855)

Didymus         *Didymi Chalcenteri fragmenta* . . . disposuit M. Schmidt (Leipzig, 1854)

Ennius          *Ennianae poesis reliquiae*: recognovit I. Vahlen[3] (Leipzig, 1903)

Epicurus        *Epicurea*: ed. H. Usener (Leipzig, 1887)

Lucilius        *C. Lucilii carminum reliquiae*: rec. F. Marx (Leipzig, 1904)

Musaeus         *Epicorum Graecorum fragmenta*: collegit G. Kinkel (Leipzig, 1877)

Orphica         *Orphicorum fragmenta*: collegit O. Kern (Berlin, 1922)

Priscian        *Institutionum grammaticarum* libri XVIII ex recensione M. Herzii (Leipzig, 1855–9)

Sallust         *C. Sallusti Crispi Historiarum reliquiae*: ed. B. Maurenbacher (Leipzig, 1891–3)

Seneca          *L. Annaei Senecae opera quae supersunt*: rec. H. Haase (Leipzig, 1852–62)

# Introduction

L. CAECILIUS Firmianus Lactantius has left us few details of his life.[1] Jerome says that he was brought up in Africa[2] and this is confirmed by his intimate familiarity with the writings of the African apologists (Tertullian, Minucius, and Cyprian), by Jerome's further comment that he was a pupil of Arnobius (at Sicca Veneria), and, perhaps, by an inscription from Cirta to a L. Caecilius Firmianus, probably from the second century. The name itself tells us little although the Caecilii Metelli were in early times patrons of North Africa.[3]

He was brought up a pagan,[4] and became a professional rhetorician, but his conversion should date to his African days.[5] Jerome says that he was summoned by Diocletian, together with a grammaticus Flavius, the author of a poetical work *De Medicinalibus*,[6] to the imperial court at Nicomedia, presumably to teach Latin and to be responsible for the Latin used in official writings.[7] To this early period Jerome ascribes a Symposium and a metrical Journey to Nicomedia, perhaps also a technical treatise entitled *Grammaticus*, none of which survives. The first extant work, dedicated to a Demetrianus,[8] to whom he also addressed two books of letters, was a small

---

[1] For the form of the names see S. Brandt, *Lactanti Opera* (Corpus Scriptorum Ecclesiasticorum Latinorum), 1.94; 2.64, 132. The facts about his life and work are discussed by R. Pichon, *Lactance* (Paris, 1901), 1–32; J. Stevenson, *Studia Patristica* 1 (1957), 661–77; P. Monat, *Institutions divines*, Livre V (Sources Chrétiennes: Paris, 1973), 1.11–15; *Prosopography of the later Roman Empire* 1.338; T. D. Barnes, *J.R.S.* 63 (1973), 29–46.

[2] *De Viris Ill.* 80.

[3] *C.I.L.* 8.7241. For other African Caecilii of the period cf. M. Caecilius Bumupal, Fl. Avianius Caecilius, consularis Numidiae, Caecilius, consiliaris of the comes Africae, Caecilius Severus Helpidius, vicarius Africae, Caecilius Cromatius Ecdicius Triumphalis, sacerdotalis Numidiae. Q. Caecilius Natalis, one of the interlocutors in Minucius Felix's *Octavius*, was a magistrate at Cirta in 210.

[4] Augustine, *De Doct. Christ.* 2.61.

[5] Note especially his familiarity with the Novatianist heresy.

[6] Also a Christian: see Jerome, *Adv. Iov.* 2.6.

[7] E. Stein, *Geschichte des spätrömischen Reiches*, 1.443–4.

[8] Otherwise unknown. Another Demetrianus was 'praefectus annonae Africae' from 369 to 372 (*P.L.R.E.* 1.247).

Christian pamphlet, *De Opificio Dei*, which marks his initiation as a Christian writer. The date is uncertain but was before the *Divine Institutions* which refers to it.[9]

The *D.I.*, a defence in seven books of Christianity, with which the present study is principally concerned, contains some decisive dating evidence, but the issues are complicated by the fact that our manuscripts preserve two editions of the work. One is represented by B (Codex Bononiensis: 5th c.), a manuscript very close in date to Lactantius himself.[10] The other edition, represented by R (Codex Parisinus Regius 1663: 9th c.), is distinguished by the addition of addresses to Constantine and by words and sentences of an overtly dualistic character. There are only two possible solutions. Either R gives the original text which was subsequently emended by Lactantius himself or a later editor. Or B gives the original text which was subsequently amplified by Lactantius himself (or a later editor).[11] Detailed examination of all the variants suggests the latter. At some period after its publication Lactantius revised, but not necessarily republished, his work in the light of his new personal situation and of his increasing commitment to dualistic theology. There are also, as we shall see, traces of alterations in his quotations of biblical and classical texts between the two versions.

The two versions can be approximately dated. Lactantius was in Nicomedia when the Great Persecution began early in A.D. 303 and remained there for at least two years (*D.I.* 5.2.2, 11.15), presumably out of office and favour. He complained of his poverty and lack of pupils (Jerome). At 5.2.2 he further implies that he was then writing at some place other than Nicomedia. Diocletian abdicated in May 305, and the presumption is that Lactantius moved to the West, Constantine's dominions, and began to compose the *D.I.* then.[12] He seems to have completed it by 311 when Galerius published

---

[9] *D.I.* 2.10.15; cf. *J.T.S.* 26 (1975), 411. See the edition by M. Perrin (Sources Chrétiènnes: Paris, 1974), 12–17.

[10] E. A. Lowe, *Codices Latini Antiquiores* (Oxford, 1938), 3, no. 180; R. W. Hunt, *Med. et Human.* 14 (1962), 3–6; P. Monat, *Rev. D'Hist. des Textes* (1975), 311–30.

[11] Pichon, *Lactance*, 28–30, suggested Lucifer Calaritanus.

[12] This is confirmed by the allusion to Hierocles (5.2.12, 4.1) who was *praeses* of Bithynia in 303: *P.L.R.E.* 1.432. The date of completion may be as late as 312; see p. 26.

his edict of toleration. The interval between the first and second editions is disputed. Stevenson[13] thought that the added invocations of Constantine (1.1.13 ff., 7.27.2 ff.) belong to the years 311–13, A. Piganiol,[14] more plausibly, suggested a date close to Constantine's execution of Licinius in 324. Most recently Heck,[15] in an exhaustive study of the problem, has given convincing grounds for dating the additions and changes to 324. Some of the impetus for the revision came from the *Epitome* which he wrote for Pentadius a long time ('iampridem') after the first edition. The Epitome contains some new reading and material, and must belong before about 320.

The revision presupposes a personal relationship with Constantine which is borne out by Jerome's note that in extreme old age Lactantius became tutor to Constantine's son Crispus in Gaul. Crispus was born about 305, proclaimed Caesar in 317, and executed in 326. Lactantius' educational activities may well belong in the years 316–20. During that same period, between the two editions, he wrote the *De Mortibus Persecutorum* (314–15) and the *De Ira* (foreshadowed in *D.I.* 2.17. 4–5). If he died in 325, he will have been born about 250, which fits with his mention of an offensive story about Cyprian which was topical in his youth (5.1.27). Cyprian was martyred in 258.

Much ingenuity has been spent on the question of the composition of the *D.I.* Stevenson argued that Books 5–7 may have been written first, under the pressure of persecution and philosophical attack, whereas the more measured Books 1–4 were composed in a less hysterical atmosphere. Yet in the form in which we have it, it is a consecutive whole. Books 5 and 6 contain references back to Books 2 and 3, and there is a clear over-all structure. Books 1–3 deal with False Religion and Wisdom, Book 4 with True Religion and Wisdom, Book 5 with Justice, Book 6 with Worship, and the apocalyptic Book 7 with the Happy Life. The total of seven books (even if, improbably, inspired by Arnobius' *Adv. Nationes*) was significant for Lactantius who attached much importance to the 'septenarius numerus', and it is difficult to believe that the basic

---

[13] See p. 1, n.1.

[14] *Rev. d'hist. et de phil. relig.* 12 (1932), 368 ff.

[15] E. Heck, *Die dualistischen Zusätze und die Kaiseranreden bei Lactantius* (Heidelberg, 1972), esp. 167 ff.

shape of the *D.I.*, with its negative and positive halves, was not in his mind from the start.

However, such questions, important as they are, are irrelevant to the present investigation which is to consider the working texts which Lactantius used. We know nothing about Lactantius' schooling, but classical education had become very stereotyped by his day. Cicero, Sallust, Terence, and Virgil were the staple diet of the schools,[16] even if an aspiring rhetorician might be expected to explore much more widely afield. Student reading, however, even when allowance is made for the far more developed memories which ancient pupils cultivated, is less to the point than the books to which Lactantius had access in his fifties and sixties when he set about his major undertaking. His method of quotation[17] shows that, although he is sometimes content to paraphrase from memory or elsewhere, he often turned to actual texts from which he copied out substantial passages. It is these which afford us the best evidence. For Lactantius travelled widely—from Africa to Nicomedia, to Gaul,[18] perhaps more than once—and ancient travel was not conducive to transporting a large collection of books with one. Nor are there likely to have been lavish library resources either at Nicomedia or at Trier, the northern capital.

Nicomedia[19] was an old city of grace and opulence, the seat of Bithynian kings and Roman governors. Its situation was vulnerable and at the same time strategic. It was sacked by the Goths in 258 and later chosen by Diocletian as an eastern capital because of its advantageous position and communications. There is a glowing account of it in Libanius, *Oration* 61, which is a lament on its destruction after the great earthquake of 358. Libanius draws attention to its many amenities—its baths, its fountains, its temples, its hippodrome, its palaces: there is no mention of a library, only a sweeping reference to μουσεῖα (61.18). Its most celebrated native was Arrian, but there is nothing to prove that he found his material in local archives. The nearest library of note was Pergamum which by

---

[16] H. I. Marrou, *A History of Education in Antiquity* (N.A.L. 1964), 374.

[17] E. Laughton, *Eranos* 49 (1951), 35 ff.

[18] His discussion of the Gallic origin of the Galatians in his letters to Probus may be relevant here (fr. 1). Also the mention of Esus and Teutates (p. 11).

[19] W. Ruge, *R.E.*, s.v.; Fergus Millar, *A Study in Cassius Dio* (Oxford, 1964), 176–7, who also mentions the Sophists Quirinus and Aelius Samius Isocrates.

300 had fallen on very hard times. One would not have found the more out-of-the-way Latin texts at Nicomędia.

Trier (Augusta Trevirorum)[20] is somewhat different. An old foundation, it was comprehensively sacked in 275 but, like Nicomedia, its strategic position, on the German frontier and on the River Moselle, made it an ideal capital in the fourth century. Constantius Chlorus rebuilt it and equipped it with fine buildings. It was essentially a manufacturing commercial centre—its wine, its armament factories, and its industries were famous. The emperors also encouraged education so that its high school acquired an enviable reputation in the West. Ausonius (*Epist.* 18) mentions two *grammatici*, Ursulus and Harmonius, from there, and an inscription (*C.I.L* 13.3702) records one 'Aemilius Epictetus grammaticus Graecus'. So too Symmachus numbered among his correspondents (*Epist.* 4.17 ff.) three former pupils from Trier—Minervius, Protadius, and Florentinus. But Ausonius and Symmachus are almost a century later than Lactantius and cannot be used as evidence for the state of learning at Trier *c.* 310. Autun, under Eumenius, was the centre of Gallic learning, rivalled by Marseilles and Bordeaux. Trier was always a frontier, military city, and it would be foolish to imagine that it could have boasted of a sophisticated classical library.

The problem of Lactantius' reading attracted earlier scholars. Pichon, in particular, devoted several chapters in his study of Lactantius, the only comprehensive biography, to examining his debt to his sources. P. de Labriolle[21] and H. Hagendahl[22] have written on the wider relationship of the Latin fathers to classical literature. There have also been many useful dissertations and articles on particular authors whom Lactantius may have read. These are cited at the appropriate point in the text. Few of them, however, analyse closely enough the context in which Lactantius gives his quotations. It is too often assumed that because he names a classical author he must have read him.

[20] Rau, *R.E.* 'Treveri'; Ewen, *Trierische höhere Schulen in Altertum* (Progr. Trier, 1884, 1894); T. J. Haarhof, *Schools of Gaul*, 48; E. M. Wightman, *Roman Trier and the Treveri* (London, 1970), 63 ff.
[21] *The History and Literature of Christianity* (London, 1924), 201 ff.
[22] *Latin Fathers and the Classics* (Göteborg, 1948).

My aim is to look in detail at his methods and techniques in the hope that the first-hand quotations can be separated from the second-hand borrowings, borrowings from other writers, compendia, anthologies, and the like. Certainty is obviously impossible, but I trust that at the end of the enquiry a very much clearer picture will have emerged of what was in Lactantius' library. It may be a modest contribution to our understanding of the culture and education of the early fourth century.[23]

[23] M. Perrin (see n. 9) has recently made an excellent analysis of the sources of the *De Opificio Dei*: see, especially, pp. 41 ff.

# I.   The Latin Poets

LACTANTIUS' knowledge of the Latin poets is perhaps the easiest element to control. We can compare his quotations in detail with the transmitted text and, because of the constrictions of verse, we can establish the degree of accuracy of the quotation. In the course of the *D.I.* he cites, by name, Cicero, Ennius, Germanicus, Horace, Juvenal, Lucan, Lucretius, Naevius, Ovid, Persius, Plautus, Propertius, Terence, and Virgil. How many of them had he actually read?

The Naevius citation, about the Fourth Sibyl, can be immediately dismissed. It is embedded in a long passage taken, ultimately, from Varro's *Divine Antiquities* (p. 52). The Juvenal one is more revealing (3.29.17), for it is the only allusion to Juvenal that Lactantius makes:

> declarat Iuvenalis his versibus:
> nullum numen habes si sit prudentia: nos te,
> nos facimus, fortuna, deam caeloque locamus.

Now the history of Juvenal's *Satires* is known. They were disregarded for 200 years and only became fashionable again at the very end of the fourth century. Ammianus (27.4.14) talks of his topicality about A.D. 390, and this can be correlated with the earliest commentary (ΣP) which mentions a Prefect of the City of 352. There is no awareness of Juvenal elsewhere in the third and early fourth centuries and the implication must be that he was rediscovered in the pagan revival associated with Julian the Apostate.[1] Lactantius' quotation is, significantly, epigrammatic: Fortune was the subject of one chapter of Stobaeus' anthology, and was ancillary to several other chapters. Did Lactantius know Juvenal, or has he got this quotation from a commonplace book which had a section on Fortune?

To answer this we have to look at his borrowings from an

---

[1] R. Syme, *Ammianus and the Historia Augusta* (Oxford, 1968), 84–8. A. Bartalucci (*S.I.F.C.* 45 (1973), 233 ff.) has challenged the accepted view by arguing that Probus, the earliest commentator on Juvenal, belongs to the early fourth century and is to be identified with Lactantius' correspondent.

earlier writer of satire, Lucilius. There are six quotations from Lucilius. One of them, about Carneades, was almost certainly taken over as a whole from Cicero's *Republic*, which provides the substance of that section of the *D.I.* (5.14.3). A second— 'illud Lucilianum: homini amico et familiari non est mentiri meum' (6.18.6)—may well have been proverbial. But the others, including several lines on Virtue, a passage believing statues to be gods, and a satirical description of a Council of the gods, are more difficult. If we only had the lines on Virtue —a favourite anthology heading—it would be natural to assume that Lactantius had taken them from some anthology, but the others are less obviously selected. Yet we know that from the third century no other writer knew Lucilius at first hand.[2] There were collections of rare words and phrases, glosses, culled from his text, and he was quoted in the commentaries on other satirists, such as Horace and Persius, but, after the archaizing fashion of the second century, he fades from view. There are only four allusions to him. Arnobius (*Adv. Nationes* 2.6) mentions grammarians who use Lucilian phrases. Ausonius quotes three words, taken from a commentary on Horace or Persius (967 Marx). Jerome refers to him twice, once in the *Commentary on Micah* (2.7—Ennius called a second Homer = 1189 Marx) and again in a letter to Chromatius (1299 Marx), likening someone eating lettuce to an ass eating thistles. The first he found in a commentary on Horace (*Epist.* 2.1.50), the second in a commentary on Cicero's *Verrines*. And that is all. Wherever Lactantius found his lines of Lucilius, it was not in Lucilius.

The passage on statues can, perhaps, be more closely determined. Lactantius is deriding the stupidity of those who hold such a belief (*stultitia*). This was a characteristically Senecan form of argument.[3] In *Epist.* 110.6 Seneca quotes two lines of Lucretius to mock them: 'quid ergo non omni puero stultiores sumus?' Elsewhere in Lactantius (2.4.14) Seneca is made to scoff the *stultitia* of the old men who believe in *pupae* dedicated to Venus (cf. Persius 2.70). Seneca may, then, be the common source.

Had he read Ennius, the father of Latin Epic poetry? There

---

[2] F. Marx, *Lucilius: Carminum Reliquiae* (Leipzig, 1904), pp. LX–LXI.
[3] See Lausberg, *Untersuchungen zu Senecas Fragmenten* (Berlin, 1972), 190–1.

are three citations from him, but a fourth, unattributed, which merely mentions a 'ferreus imber' could as easily be inspired by Virgil (*Aen.* 12.284) as by Ennius. One of them—'pellitur e medio sapientia, vi geritur res'—was famous (5.1.5). It is used by Cicero (*Pro Murena* 30), although the manuscript tradition of Cicero is very corrupt, giving 'tollitur' or 'bellitur' instead of 'pellitur' and 'videtur res(pernitur)' instead of 'vi geritur res'. It also is quoted by Aulus Gellius (20.10.4).

The other two quotations, attributed by name to Ennius, are more difficult. The first records (1.15.31) the talk among the Roman bystanders at the apotheosis of Romulus ( = Vahlen 1.115–18). It was a celebrated passage: the grammarian Priscian (1.262 K.) quotes a line of it, but the five lines in question are also quoted by Cicero in his *De Republica* (1.64), and the *De Republica* is a major source of Lactantius' Roman history. It is cited more than thirty-five times. It is true that there are small divergences between Cicero's and Lactantius' texts, but they, as we shall see again when dealing with Lactantius' use of the poet Lucretius, may be due to no more than failure of memory or the use of a different text of the *De Republica* from the palimpsest which is our sole authority. The significant variant is 'o pater, o patriae' for 'o pater, o genitor', but the phrase 'pater patriae' was almost dangerously familiar: it was one of the Emperor's titles. The second passage is an epigram spoken by Scipio:

> si fas endo plagas caelestum ascendere cuiquam est
> mi soli caeli maxima porta patet.

The manuscripts of Lactantius in fact (apart from H) read 'faciendo' instead of 'fas endo', because *endo* is an archaic and obscure word (1.18.11). In the context Lactantius makes it clear that once again he is drawing on Cicero ('cui vanitati Cicero adsensit') but the origin of the quotation is put beyond doubt by Seneca who writes in a letter (108.34): 'esse enim apud Ciceronem in his ipsis de republica libris hoc epigramma' —and quotes the two lines. One of Seneca's manuscripts gives the true reading 'fas endo', the other (Q) reads 'fascendo' which is half way to Lactantius' 'faciendo'. Ennius' works were no longer known after the time of Fronto in the second century, and subsequent quotations in grammarians were derived either from encyclopedias or school-selections, or other secondary sources.[4]

Lucan and Propertius are equally doubtful, although for different reasons. It used to be argued[5] that Propertius was not read during the Roman Empire and was only rediscovered in the Renaissance. Enk and Shackleton Bailey[6] have disputed this and traced his influence in such writers as Claudian, Sedulius, and Dracontius. So it is not out of the question that Lactantius could have read a copy of his poems. But he quotes him only once (2.6.14)—four lines on the subject of Romulus and his senate (Prop. 4. 1.11–14). And those four lines are also used by Isidore (18.4.1) as an illustration of the rare word *buccina*. This coincidence certainly indicates a derivative, second-hand source for the quotation—in Lactantius' case possibly Seneca again.

The Lucan example is odder. Lactantius names him only once (1.21.20) but the quotation that he gives 'numquamque satis quaesitus Osiris') does not come from Lucan but from Ovid, *Metam.* 9. 693. In the following paragraph he does indeed quote two lines of Lucan (9.158–9), part of the speech of the young Pompey on hearing of the death of his father—but the lines are unattributed. They refer to the Egyptian deities Isis and Osiris:

> evolvam busto iam numen gentibus Isim
> et tectum lino spargam per vulgus Osirim.

They were evidently famous lines because they are imitated by Claudian. But while Lactantius may well have had first-hand information about Isis and Osiris—he was after all an African and a well-travelled man—he makes a strange mistake. He calls Osiris the son of Isis (1.17.6) but, as is well known, Osiris was the husband not the son of Isis. The only other author to make this mistake is Minucius (23.1 'Isis perditum filium luget, plangit, inquirit') and Minucius was one of Lactantius' chief inspirations. And so the combination of a wrongly attributed quotation and a mistake about the identity of Osiris

---

[4] Müller, *Quintus Ennius* (St. Petersburg, 1884), 274. On the Scipio passage see also S. Weinstock, *Divus Iulius* (Oxford, 1971), 294 n. 10.

[5] e.g. by F. Pléssis, *Études critiques sur Properce* (Paris, 1884), 300.

[6] P. J. Enk, *Monobiblos* (Leiden, 1946), 55–77; D. R. Shackleton Bailey, *Propertiana* (Cambridge, 1956), 268 ff.

leads me to doubt very seriously whether Lactantius possessed a copy of Lucan at all. The quotation is either due to a second-ary source or to a garbled childhood memory. Perhaps the latter, for, at 1.21.2–3, talking of human sacrifice, he mentions the sacrifices performed to Diana 'apud Tauros', to Esus and Teutates among the Gauls, and to Juppiter Latiaris at Rome. This last may have been an apologetic commonplace (cf. Tertullian, *Scorp.* 7.6; Porph. *De Abstin.* 2.56), but Esus and Teutates elsewhere only figure in Lucan 1.444–5.[7]

> et quibus immitis placatur sanguine diro
> Teutates horrensque feris altaribus Esus

and the following line includes Scythian Taranis (Diana)— 'et Taranis Scythicae non mitior ara Dianae'. Nevertheless both Lucan and Lactantius include further examples not in each other and there is no hint of direct consultation of Lucan in the passage.

Of the great comic poets Plautus is quoted twice:

> sua sibi habent regna reges, suas divitias divites

and the *sententia* (as Lactantius calls it)

> male meretur qui mendico dat quod edat:
> nam et illut quod dat perit et illi producit
> vitam ad miseriam

(*D.I.* 5.12.11, 6.11.8). Does this mean that Lactantius knew and read Plautus? Certainly not, because the second quotation has been tailored and adapted to make a suitable adage. The true text of Plautus (*Trin.* 339–40) has the less usual *prodit* instead of *producit* and adds the superfluous *aut bibat* (food or drink). We see here what is a familiar tendency, the adaptation of a passage to make it more memorable, more quotable.

Terence is much more difficult.[8] Five of the six quotations are indeed proverbial. One of them (3.18.13 = *Heaut. Tim.* 971–2) shows the kind of simplification which has been discussed above and which was typical of the commonplace book:

> prius quaeso disce quid sit vivere,
> ubi scies, si displicebit vita, tum istoc utitor.

---

[7] Lucan, *De Bello Civili* I, ed. R. J. Getty (Cambridge, 1940), Appendix D.
[8] See T. D. Barnes, *Tertullian* (Oxford, 1971), 196.

Lactantius wrote:

> prius disce quid sit vivere:
> si displicebit vita, tum istoc utitur.

> utitur SH: utitor PV: utito B *ras.*

Another—'suo sibi gladio' (3.28.20 = *Adelph.* 958)—is also
quoted by Cicero (*Pro Caec.* 82), Ambrose (*De Off.* 1.15) and
Publilius Syrus. The third—'milder than a sheep' (3.26.4—
*Adelph.* 534; Lactantius alters *reddo* to *reddam* for the syntax)—
is similarly proverbial and is quoted by Sulpicius Severus (*Dial.*
2.9.4) and alluded to by Apuleius (*Met.* 7.23). The fourth—
'veritas odium parit' (5.9.6 = *Andria* 68)—is even more self-
evident. Augustine (*ap.* Jerome, *Epist.* 116.31) called it a common proverb, and it is used by Cicero (*De Amicitia* 89), Sulpicius Severus (1.9.3), Rufinus (p. 559 Keil), and no less than
three times by Isidore (2.9.11, 11.1, 21.16). The fifth—one
sees other people's faults better than one's own—is of the same
kind. Although not explicitly quoted by Cicero, it is referred
to by him twice (*De Off.* 1.146; *Tusc. Disp.* 3.73) in language
which makes it clear that he is paraphrasing a familiar saying
of Terence's, and Seneca in one of his letters (*Epist.* 109.16)
also gives a nearly word-for-word recollection of it. But the
final example does not have the same pedigree (*D.I.* 7.27.3 =
*Phormio* 249 'molendum esse in pistrino, vapulandum: habendae
compedes'). So the Codex Bembinus. Later manuscripts insert
*mihi* or *mihi usque* (CFL[2]: PD[2]E) against the metre. Lactantius
adds *usque* alone and in so doing shows that he knew an inter-
polated text but not the text that is represented in our
surviving tradition. The line does not appear to be quoted
elsewhere. Yet, in face of the evidence, one can only doubt
whether Lactantius was really familiar with Terence's plays.
Five out of the six quotations are proverbial, and can be proved
to be so. The sixth could easily be, and I suspect was. Yet
such a conclusion is very surprising. Terence enjoyed great
popularity in the schools of the late Empire. Jerome was to
read his plays at Rome under the tuition of Aelius Donatus
himself who wrote a magisterial commentary on Terence. And
the Bembine manuscript dates from this century. Furthermore
it is usually assumed that the Firmianus, who discussed questions of Terentian metre in a work addressed to Probus (Brandt

fr. 2), was Lactantius, but this is not wholly secure. He may be the same as the commentator on Virgil, mentioned by Servius, but distinct from Lactantius.

We are then left with Ovid, Horace, Lucretius, Virgil, Persius, and the Latin versions of Aratus' *Phaenomena*. Aratus, a contemporary of Theocritus and Callimachus, wrote in Greek a didactic poem on the stars, a versification of a prose treatise by Eudoxus. For all its faults Aratus' poem enjoyed great popularity. Jerome (*In Tit.* 1.12) speaks of very many translations of it and we know of versions by Varro of Atax, Cicero, Ovid, Germanicus, Avienus, and, doubtfully, the Emperor Gordian. There were also more than twenty-seven commentaries written on it. The translations by Cicero and Germanicus[9] were still read in the fourth century (Priscian 3.417 K.; Firm. *Math.* 8.5; Calpurnius Siculus 4.1; Claudian, *Paneg. de VI Hon.* 171 ff.; *In Eutrop.* 2.165) and, together with Avienus, survived in manuscripts down to the late Middle Ages. Now Lactantius first of all mentions 'ii qui phaenomena conscripserunt' (1.21.28) for an explanation why the two stars of Cancer are called ὄνοι (asses) and then, a few sections later, quotes four lines of Germanicus (165–8) on the suckling of Juppiter by a Cretan goat. He follows them immediately by an allusion to Musaeus, a mythical poet, to whom was attributed a theogony, which was in fact probably written in sixth-century-B.C. Athens: 'huius capellae corio usum esse pro scuto Iovem contra Titanas dimicantem'. Musaeus is only here mentioned by Lactantius and the connection of Musaeus and Germanicus is significant, because one of the few verbatim quotations of Musaeus (fr. 7 Kinkel: Ps.-Eratosthenes, *Catast.* 13.11) is three lines on Zeus being reared by Amalthea and the goat.[10] Those lines are adapted by Germanicus (157 ff.) in a departure from Aratus' text, and are commented on by one of the ancient commentators (ΣStrozz.) on Germanicus' poems. The issue is put beyond doubt by another fragment of Musaeus (fr. 12 Kinkel) on the Hyades, which is preserved once again by the

---

[9] The latest edition, with a full bibliography, is by D. B. Gain (Athlone Press, 1976), who argues that the poem might equally have been written by Germanicus' uncle, the Emperor Tiberius.

[10] The same allusion to Musaeus is made by Theophilus (*Ad Autol.* 1.9). R. M. Grant (*J.T.S.* 26 (1975), 186–9) argues that Theophilus was drawing on Chrysippan material derived immediately from Clitomachus: but see p. 7.

Σ on Germanicus (*Aratea* 174 ff.). In other words there was an ancient commentary on Germanicus' *Aratea* which contained parallels from Musaeus. The three other lines from Germanicus (112,113,137) occur in a single chapter (*D.I.* 5.5): there they are compared with two passages of Cicero (*Arat.* frs. 21,23), which are Lactantius' only references to Cicero's *Aratea*. This again points to the work of a commentator rather than the separate reading of Cicero's poems by Lactantius. And it can surely be no coincidence that the lines from Ovid's translation, which is otherwise only known from a single reference in the grammarian Probus (on Virgil, *Georg.* 1.138), are the final three lines. Beginnings and ends are the stuff of commentaries. My conclusion then is that Lactantius knew a commentary on Aratus, from which he derived the Germanicus quotations as well. Such books did exist and were standard textbooks, as the surviving works by Hyginus show.[11]

In the world of late antiquity, as in the Middle Ages and the Renaissance, indeed as in educated Europe down to the nineteenth century, memory played a much greater part in the recall and use of poetry. When, therefore, we try to analyse an author's sources, when we try to see what texts he was using and what relationship they bear to the texts that have survived down to modern times, we have constantly to remember the inherent perils of the undertaking. Lactantius was quoting for the point of the quotation, not for its precise text or language, and we have to exercise extreme caution in using his evidence for the restoration of a classical text. Leaving aside all the obvious cases where he has tailored his quotation to fit the syntax of his own sentence, one can show that there are many places where he has substituted a more common or more contemporary word or form for the original. Where Ovid, for instance, discusses the creation of man and his upright stance (*Met.* 1.85–6), he says that the creator ordered man to look upwards to the sky. Ovid writes:

> caelumque tueri
> iussit.

---

[11] For ancient Latin commentaries J. E. G. Zetzel, *H.S.C.P.* 79 (1975), 335 ff. who draws attention to their widespread popularity in the later fourth and fifth centuries. Jerome had read commentaries on Plautus, Lucretius, Horace, Persius, Virgil, Sallust, and Cicero.

Lactantius substituted *videre* for the rarer *tueri*. Describing the arrival of Saturn at the river Tiber, Ovid says 'venit in amnem'; Lactantius (with some of the later manuscripts of Ovid) the more normal 'venit ad amnem'. Quoting Persius, once again on man's upright stance, Lactantius writes 'o curvae in terras mentes' (2.2.18 = 2.61) for 'o curvae in terris mentes'. The accusative of motion is more natural. This tendency to trivialize or normalize is particularly evident in his way of quoting from Lucretius—his second most favoured Roman poet. Excluding passages quoted more than once, the figures are ninety-one citations from Virgil and sixty-two from Lucretius, compared with thirty-one from Ovid and only eight from Horace. The statistics are interesting in themselves, but whereas there is no case of such trivialization at all from Virgil, there are at least six from Lucretius, involving such things as replacing *nil* by the usual *nihil* (1.159, 1.205), *gerere* by *agere* (5.167), *tramite* by *limite*, the archaic *vertier* by *vertere se* (5.1199). Clearest of all is where he alters Lucretius' 'terram radicibus apti' to 'terrae radicibus apti' (2.11.1 = 5.808). A similar instance occurs in Horace. Nothing, says Horace (*Odes* 3.3.1–4), shakes the just man from his firmness of purpose—'mente quatit solida'. The ablative is perhaps not immediately easy to understand, and for that reason Lactantius simplifies it to 'mentem quatit solidam'. There can be no question of the transmission of Lactantius' reading being at fault: we are fortunate in having texts which go back almost to the author himself. Some of these variants may simply be due to carelessness or faulty memory; indeed it is hard to explain otherwise the unmetrical lines which occasionally result, e.g. *mentem* in Horace or *agere* in Lucretius. Such metrical violations are unexpected in an author who may himself have been the author of a substantial poem and was certainly familiar with the principles of Latin versification. Yet he seems to have included *saepe* against the metre as part of a quotation from Lucretius 1.83. He certainly had no authority for substituting *fulgentia* for *rellatum* in Lucretius 2.1001: here he is probably recalling other phrases in which *fulgens* is associated with the starry sky (e.g. Lucr. 6.357). So too, quoting Lucretius' contempt for the inaccuracy of Juppiter's thunderbolt (2.1101–2)

aedes

saepe suas disturbet,

he writes *ipse* instead of *saepe* because of the common collocation *ipse su(as)* in Latin. The occurrence of *sed* for *et* (2.1000), *nec* for *et* (5.1200), *primum* for *primus* (5.536) and the omission of small words like *est* (Verg. *Georg.* 3.112) all point to the same hurried quotation from memory.

But when all that has been said, his generous quotation from the classics does shed a great deal of light on several important matters, in particular on the text of certain individual passages, on the history of the transmission of various authors and on what Latin literature was read in his lifetime.

It is generally assumed that our main witnesses for the text of Lucretius, the Oblongus and Quadratus manuscripts of the Carolingian period, are ultimately derived from a fourth- or fifth-century manuscript, now lost, written in uncials in France. In at least two places Lactantius preserves the true reading, hardly by his own conjecture, and, therefore, used an earlier state of the tradition. At 3.1044 OQ call the sun *aerius*: Lactantius quoting the line writes *aetherius*, the adjective which Lucretius uses elsewhere for the sun (5.215, 267, 281, 389). There is little semantic difference, but *aerius* happens not to be used of the sun and so Lactantius is correct. At 2.1000 OQ have the unmetrical 'quod missus ex aetheris oris': Lactantius preserves the true 'missum est', which was conjectured by much later copyists of Lucretius.

The history of Virgil is a royal progress. Substantial fragments of a fine text survive from the third century and the main manuscript—the Mediceus—dates from the fifth. The text is very largely secure and authoritative: there are few variants or corruptions in it. As one would expect Lactantius' quotations reflect the state of the late classical text and such departures as there are are chiefly due to trivialization (*Georg.* 4.200) or carelessness (*Georg.* 3.112). A good example of this is where Lactantius substitutes 'permixtus' for the rarer 'commixtus' (1.5.19 = *Georg.* 2.327). There is however one passage which may throw some further light on the scene. Lactantius made two editions of the *Institutes* (reflected by the manuscripts B and R). At *Aen.* 4.464–5, Dido is tortured by supernatural occurrences after Aeneas has made his escape from Carthage, and she is terrified by the memory of frightening prophecies ( = *D.I.* 2.17.2):

    multaque praeterea vatum praedicta priorum
    . . . horrificant.

*Priorum* or *piorum*? Both readings were known to Servius, and the Mediceus has *piorum* while other early manuscripts have *priorum*, which is generally preferred by editors. It seems that Lactantius also knew both readings, because in the first edition he wrote *piorum* (RPV), in the second *priorum* (BH). The same phenomenon can be detected, though less certainly, in a few other places (*Ecl.* 4.28 flavescet S: flavescit B; 4.42 discet S: discit BHP; cf. *Aen.* 6.735,750).[12]

    A rather different pattern emerges from an investigation of the Ovid quotations.[13] It is strange that he quotes only from the *Fasti* and the *Metamorphoses* (the supposed reference to the *Letters from Pontus* is no more than a proverb: 6.17.11 = *Ex Pont.* 3.1.35).[14] There was plenty of suitable material in the *Amores* or the *Heroides* or the *Tristia*, but he seems not to have known them. Our text of the Fasti stems from a split tradition, represented by a Vatican manuscript (A) of the tenth century on the one hand, and a group of three manuscripts (UGM) on the other, the two branches being distinguished by significant errors and omissions. There is one passage (4.209 'pars clipeos sudibus, galeas pars tundit inanes') where Lactantius is the only authority to preserve *sudibus*; the Ovid manuscripts have either *manibus* (AU; cf. *Heroides* 3.119) or *rudibus* (GM). Unfortunately at 6.294 where Ovid's manuscripts are divided between the correct *amat* (GM), which Lactantius also read (1.12.6), and the incorrect *habet* (cf. 298), one of the main branches of the Ovid tradition (A) is missing. However, it does seem clear from these and other passages that Lactantius' copy of the *Fasti* predates the splitting of the manuscript tradition into its present groups.

    It is different with the *Metamorphoses*. Here again there are two main groups of manuscripts—one (MNU), lacking Book

[12] But the Firmianus quoted by Servius, *Ad Aen.* 7.543 for the correction *convecta* for *convexa* may not be Lactantius. See J. Stevenson, *Studia Patristica* 1 (1957), 671. Note also P. Monat, *Ant. Class.* 43 (1974), 346–54.

[13] See also L. Alfonsi, *Vig. Christ.* 14 (1960), 170–6.

[14] See Kraus, *R.E.*, 'Ovidius'. *D.I.* 3.24.6 *might* be derived from Ovid, *Fasti* 6.271–6, which are missing from all the manuscripts except U, but probably not directly, since the whole passage does not seem to depend on Ovid. See, however, Lenz, *Rend. Accad. Lincei* 6 (1937), 365 ff.

15 and containing fifth-century prose summaries, and a second, containing Book 15 but not the summaries, and further distinguished by separate errors. In two places Lactantius' readings show marked affinity with the first group. At *Met.* 1.173–4 ('a fronte potentes caelicolae'), N and Lactantius (1.16.12) read *hac fronte*. At *Met.* 1.258 ('mundi moles obsessa laboret') MN have *proles* for *moles*; Lactantius (*De Ira* 23.6) instead of *moles obsessa* read *moles operosa*, a corruption resulting from the addition of *pr*, intended to alter *moles* to *proles*. Nor does Lactantius have any quotation from Book 15. It looks, therefore, as if the manuscript tradition of the *Metamorphoses* was already divided and that Lactantius knew the first branch.

At 3.17.14 he quotes three lines from Cicero's poem on his Consulship. These lines are quoted twice by Cicero himself in the *De Divinatione*, once in the middle of a long section of the poem (1.19) and once as a triplet on their own (2.45). Lactantius does not specify his immediate source ('in libris consulatus sui eadem dixit quae Lucretius'; the *De Divinatione* is not mentioned in the context and is barely cited by Lactantius elsewhere; see p. 69), but the version that he gives contains a significant variation in the second line ('ipse suas arces atque incluta templa petivit' for 'ipse suos quondam tumulos ac templa petivit'). There is no obvious explanation, palaeographically or otherwise: the conjunction 'incluta templa' does not occur elsewhere. But we know that there were two versions of the poem, one published about 55 B.C. and one some years earlier (see Pease's note on *De Div.* 1.19) and it is therefore a reasonable hypothesis that Lactantius' lines are from the earlier version which Cicero, with his liking for alliteration (e.g. 'fixa ac fundata') improved. But it would be straining credulity to believe that Lactantius had a copy of the actual poem. He must have found it in some other work. The fact that Cicero quotes these three lines twice is proof that he was proud of them.

Finally Lactantius does not specify whether the 'quidam poeta' who wrote a Triumph of Love (1.11.1–2), in which Juppiter and the other gods are led in chains in front of his chariot, was Greek or Roman.[15] There is some parallelism with

---

[15] Phanocles: R. Förster, *Der Raub und die Rückkehr der Persephone*, 85 n. 2; Artemidorus: E. Rohde, *Roman*, 115 n. 1; E. Reitzenstein, *Rh. Mus.* 84 (1935), 75n.

the image used by Ovid (*Amores* 1.2.23 ff.) and a Hellenistic poem has been inferred. The Roman character of the poem seems indicated by the detailed description of the triumph, but this may be colouring from a Latin paraphrase, for it is certain from the vagueness of 'quidam poeta' that Lactantius had not read an original poem. Indeed it may be no accident that Artemidorus who wrote elegies on Eros is quoted by the $\Sigma$ on Germanicus' *Aratea* (320; cf. Ps.-Eratosthenes p. 158 on Amphitrite, Neptune, and the Dolphin).[16] Once again we come back to commentaries on the *Aratea*.

[16] E. Maass, *Aratea* (Philologische Untersuchungen 12 (1892)), 325–6.

# II. Greek Poetry

LACTANTIUS' knowledge and use of Greek poets is a much simpler task to undertake, apart from the special questions posed by the *Orphica* and the *Carmina Sibyllina*. He refers to only four poets—Homer, Hesiod, Euripides, and Musaeus.

Euripides, mentioned twice, is never quoted in Greek. The first reference, to the prologue of the *Lamia*, which alluded to a Libyan Sibyl (1.6.9), comes in the passage about the nine Sibyls which stems from Varro. The second is an epigrammatic remark translated into Latin—'quae hic mala putantur, haec sunt in caelo bona' (5.15.11). We do not know of any Latin translations of Euripides and there is no precise equivalent of the line in Euripides' extant plays. It may however be a free paraphrase of *Ion* 449–451 (so Wilamowitz, *Anal. Eurip.*, 22) and significantly that passage was used in Christian apologetics earlier by Ps.-Justin Martyr (*De Monarch.* 5). This suggests a common rhetorical source. Brandt lists a third quotation (*Polyid.* fr. 639 N. τίς δ' οἶδεν εἰ τὸ ζῆν μέν ἐστι κατθανεῖν / τὸ κατθανεῖν δὲ ζῆν = 3.19.13), identifying our life with death, but Lactantius does not cite Euripides and, in the immediate context, he has drawn the epigram directly from Cicero (*De Rep.* 6.14, a work much consulted at this point of *D.I.*). Nothing then points to first-hand acquaintance with Euripides.

The same can be said about Hesiod. Lactantius knew that he had written a *Theogony* and gives a very bald résumé of it (1.5.8, 10), but he does not quote from the text. On the other hand he does correctly quote two lines of the *Works and Days* (122–3 = 2.14.7) in a long discussion on demons. However, as we shall see later, the whole of this section is taken over from a source very close to Minucius Felix (26.8 ff.), who was in turn inspired by Tertullian (*Apol.* 22). Lactantius, like his two predecessors, quotes Plato and poets for the existence of demons—'omnes poetae sciunt, philosophi disserunt'. And there is a long history behind the connection of Hesiod's lines with demonology, going back to Plato's *Cratylus* 398, who gives the same etymology of δαίμων as Lactantius, and later grammarians such as Hesychius and apologists such as Augustine, *C.D.* 9.21 (from δαήμων 'skilful'). Plato quotes lines 122 and 123 in a variant version:

> οἱ μὲν δαίμονες ἁγνοὶ ὑποχθόνιοι καλέονται,
> ἐσθλοί, ἀλεξίκακοι, φύλακες θνητῶν ἀνθρώπων.

The lines were much quoted and parodied (Sext. Emp. p. 175.1; D.L. 9.73) and had long been part of apologetic armoury (Origen, *C. Cels.* 7.50; Clement, *Strom.* 3 p. 517). The proof of this lies in the fact that Theodoret, who certainly did not know Lactantius, not only has the *Cratylus* δαίμων–δαήμων definition but also quotes the three lines of Hesiod, again in a slightly variant text (*Therapeut.* 8.47):

> αὐτὰρ ἐπειδὴ τοῦτο γένος κατὰ μοῖρ' ἐκάλυψεν,
> οἱ μὲν δαίμονες ἁγνοὶ ἐπιχθόνιοι καλέονται,
> ἐσθλοί, ἀλεξίκακοι, φύλακες θνητῶν ἀνθρώπων.

The passage, therefore, became part of the stock tradition and is quoted three times by Plutarch in his, very similar, accounts of demons (*De Def.* 417 B, 431 E; *Isis* 361 B), again with a variant in line 122 ἁγνοί, ἐπιχθόνιοι. Lactantius can hardly have used the passage from his own, personal familiarity with the *Works and Days*.

It is to such demonological works that one allusion to Homer will also belong (4.27.15 'credant Homero qui summum illum Iovem daemonibus adgregavit' = *Iliad* 1.222). More interesting is his passing reference to Homer's belief that Castor and Pollux were mortal (*Iliad* 3.243 = 1.10.6). Here he does indeed quote a line but in a Latin verse translation:

> haec ait, ast illos retinebat terra sepultos.

We know of several Latin translations: from the Republic those of Cn. Matius and Ninius Crassus, from the early Empire those of Polybius (a freedman of Claudius), Attius Labeo (Pers. *Sat.* 1.4, but it was *verbum ex verbo*), and the abbreviated *Ilias Latina*. There will have been others, but it is unlikely that Lactantius made the translation himself and equally unlikely, therefore, that he knew the original. The third comes in a discussion of the name of Christ—the anointed (*unctus*). The derivation was a commonplace of apologetics (cf. Tertullian,

*Apol.* 3.5 'Christianus . . . de unctione deducitur'; Justin, *Dial.* 49.1, 86.3, Hippolytus, *Dan.* 4.32.4, etc.). Lactantius adds that χρίεσθαι in ancient Greek meant ἀλείφεσθαι 'sicut indicat Homeri versus ille' (4.7.7):

> τοὺς δ' ἐπεὶ οὖν δμῳαὶ λοῦσαν καὶ χρῖσαν ἐλαίῳ

(= *Od.* 4.49).

Did Lactantius make the connection for himself? I think not. The context is one of obvious polemic, especially against Greek translators who preferred ἠλειμμένος as a translation of the Hebrew Messiah. The passage is one of several anti-Jewish pieces of exegesis in Book 4 which must have a common source. I have not found the line itself quoted elsewhere for this purpose, but if Lactantius had really been so familiar with Homer, one would expect him to quote more extensively.

Oracles were traditionally communicated in verse. In the Empire the main oracular seat of Apollo was no longer at Delphi but at Claros in Asia Minor (cf. *D.I.* 1.7.1) and under neo-Platonic influence the oracle was popularizing a spiritual monotheism of an impressive character. Some fragmentary inscriptions have recently been found which supplement the very extensive quotations which can be recovered, largely from Eusebius' *Praep. Evang.* and the Tübingen *Theosophy*,[1] of the collection which Porphyry made in the middle of the third century for his περὶ τῆς ἐκ λογίων φιλοσοφίας.[2]

Lactantius quotes six, excluding the 'Dodona' oracle which is discussed later (p. 25). In one Apollo is said to be 'Colophone respondens' (1.7.1: *residens* Brandt), in another he is called Apollo Smintheus (1.7.9), in two others Apollo Milesius (4.13.11, 7.13.5) and in two others simply, Apollo. They merit individual consideration.

1. 1.7.1. quaerenti quis aut quid esset omnino deus, respondit XXI versibus, quorum hoc principium est:

> αὐτοφυὴς ἀδίδακτος ἀμήτωρ ἀστυφέλικτος,
> οὔνομα μηδὲ λόγῳ χωρούμενος, ἐν πυρὶ ναίων,
> τοῦτο θεός, μικρὰ δὲ θεοῦ μερὶς ἄγγελοι ἡμεῖς.

These lines occur as the concluding three lines of a sixteen-line oracle in the *Theosophy* ( = Buresch no. 13) where the additional

---

[1] H. Erbse, *Fragmente griech. Theosophien* (Hamburg, 1941).
[2] G. Wolff, *Porphyrii de Philosophia* (Berlin, 1856); K. Buresch, *Klaros* (1889).

fact is given that the reply was made to a certain Theophilus asking σὺ εἶ θεὸς ἢ ἄλλος.[3] Editors have therefore emended *principium* to *praecipuum* (Wolff) or understand it as meaning 'sum, total' (Buresch: impossible, cf. 4.6.5), but the variation between sixteen and twenty-one lines suggests some difference in the two texts in any case. Recently, however, epigraphic confirmation of the oracle has been recognized at Oenoanda[4] where the three lines (with the theologically important μὴ χωρῶν, πολυώνυμος for μηδὲ λόγῳ χωρούμενος) were inscribed on the rampart and followed by

τοῦτο πευθομένοισι θεοῦ πέρι ὅστις ὑπάρχει
Αἰ[θ]έ[ρ]α πανδερκ[ῆ] θεοῦ ἔννεπεν, εἰς ὃν ὁρῶντες
εὔχεσθ' ἠῴους πρὸς ἀντολίην ἐσορῶντας

(which are not quoted in the *Theosophy*).

So Theophilus came from Oenoanda and the oracle was a real one, the substitution of χωρούμενος being aimed to get rid of πολυώνυμος unacceptable to Christian monotheism. The citizens of Oenoanda only inscribed the three crucial lines—they may, therefore, have been detached on the original, which would explain their different position in Lactantius and the *Theosophy*—and the actual prescription for prayer. Lactantius will have found it in a Christian anthology compiled from Porphyry, since the Christian χωρούμενος is common to him and the *Theosophy* and since he himself shows no direct knowledge of Porphyry's work.

2. 1.7.9   πάνσοφε παντοδίδακτε πολύστροφε κέκλυθι δαῖμον.

3. 1.7.9   ἁρμονίη κόσμοιο, φαεσφόρε, πάνσοφε δαῖμον.

4. 1.7.10  δαίμονες οἳ φοιτῶσι περὶ χθόνα καὶ περὶ πόντον
            ἀκαμάτου δαμνῶνται ὑπαὶ μάστιγι θεοῖο.

No comparable parallels exist for these three fragments but παντοδίδακτος occurs in another oracle, describing Plutonis (Phlegon 36 J.) and the second line of 4 recalls Proclus, *Hymn. in Sol.* 27

δειμαίνουσι δὲ σεῖο θοῆς μάστιγος ἀπειλήν/δαίμονες.

The language, therefore, looks authentic.

---

[3] For the question see Dodds, *Pagan and Christian in an Age of Anxiety*, 57; A. D. Nock, *Essays*, 1.160 ff.

[4] L. Robert, *C.R.A.I.* (1971), 597 ff. Earlier discussion in P. Batiffol, *Rev. bibl.* 25 (1916), 177 ff.

5. 4.13.11   consultus utrumne deus an homo fuerit

> θνητὸς ἔην κατὰ σάρκα σοφὸς τερατώδεσιν ἔργοις
> ἀλλ' ὑπὸ Χαλδαίοισι δικασπολίαισιν ἁλώσας
> γομφωθεὶς σκολόπεσσι πικρὴν ἀνέπλησε τελευτήν.

This, as Wolff (183 ff.) saw, has a close affinity to Augustine, *C.D.* 19.23, who quotes Porphyry for an oracle of Apollo, '. . . mortuum deum cantans quem a iudicibus recta sentientibus perditum, pessima in speciosis ferro iuncta mors interfecit.' Both oracles were certainly not the work of Christians and their similarity suggests that they were collected from extant copies (? at Claros) by Porphyry.[5]

6. 7.13.5   Polites quidam consuluit utrumne maneat anima post mortem an dissolvatur, et respondit his versibus:

> ψυχὴ μὲν μέχρις οὗ δεσμοῖς πρὸς σῶμα κρατεῖται,
> φθαρτὰ νοοῦσα πάθη θνηταῖς ἀλγηδόσιν εἴκει·
> ἡνίκα δ' ἀνάλυσιν βροτέην μετὰ σῶμα μαρανθέν
> ὠκίστην εὕρηται, εἰς αἰθέρα πᾶσα φορεῖται
> αἰὲν ἀγήραος οὖσα, μένει δ' εἰς πάμπαν ἀτειρής.
> πρωτόγονος γὰρ τοῦτο θεία διέταξε πρόνοια.

Here again the language is authentic: μετὰ σῶμα μαρανθέν occurs in an oracle of Apollonius of Tyana (Philostratus 8.31) and the idea of the soul going to the air is Platonic and would have appealed to Porphyry.

The clues all fit together. Porphyry compiled a major collection of genuine oracles from which he drew important philosophical conclusions. That work was known to Augustine. A Christianized redaction of it was used by Lactantius and the author of the *Theosophy*, and, perhaps first of all for apologetic purposes, Arnobius. Lactantius himself had not studied the originals.[6]

The oracle at 1.21.7 is different. Lactantius is discussing human sacrifice and claims that it existed even at Rome, with the ceremony of throwing people from the Milvian Bridge:

---

[5] Augustine (*C.D.* 19.23) also gives a Latin paraphrase of another oracle about the Jews, three lines of which are quoted in Greek by Lactantius (*De Ira* 23.12).

But Dodds (*H.T.R.* 54 (1961), 285) rightly points out that the collector of the *Theosophy* only calls two oracles (27+29, and 30) Porphyrian, implying that he may have found the others elsewhere; on the other hand there is another significantly common link between Lactantius and the *Theosophy* in Varro's list of Sibyls: see p. 54.

'Quod ex responso quodam factitatum Varro auctor est: cuius responsi ultimus versus est talis:

καὶ κεφαλὰς Ἀΐδῃ καὶ τῷ πατρὶ πέμπετε φῶτα.

In the epitome of this passage (18.2) the oracle is said to have been given 'ex persona Apollinis'.

Now this oracle was a famous one which is quoted at length by D.H. 1.19.3 (from Varro) and Macrobius (*Sat.* 1.7.28). It is also alluded to by Arnobius (*Adv. Nat.* 2.68 'cum ex Apollinis monitu patri Diti ac Saturno humanis capitibus supplicaretur'. But there are three oddities about the passage.

1. The earliest tradition made it an oracle of Zeus at Dodona; as such it was discussed by L. Manlius, a Sullan writer (D.H.). And it was as an oracle of Zeus that it was regarded by Varro (D.H., Macrobius), Verrius Flaccus (Festus 450 L.), and Ovid (*Fasti* 5.625 ff.). Why then the mention of Apollo? Apollo was originally not associated in any capacity with Dodona, but from the early empire onwards confusion set in. Strabo (7.1.1) speaks of the oracle of Apollo at Dodona and the author of the *Aetna* (6) names Dodona as a favourite haunt of Apollo. E. Bickel[7] argued that because of the decline of the cult of Zeus at Dodona, Apollo, as the oracular god *par excellence*, became generally associated with the now defunct centre—a transference which Cornelius Labeo may have encouraged. But, as Goodyear points out,[8] the evidence is very slight and neither Arnobius nor Lactantius actually mentions Dodona. Since both authors seem to have used a Christian Anthology of Clarian oracles derived from Porphyry, it may be that the mistake was made at that point, a mistake inspired by the mention of Phoebus in the penultimate line.

2. Lactantius and Macrobius quote the last line with Ἀΐδῃ, D.H. with Κρονίδῃ: all three claim the authority of Varro. D.H. is likely to have reported Varro accurately and Ἀΐδῃ is by way of a trivialization. That fact again indicates that Lactantius derived it from a secondary source and not from Varro himself.

3. Lactantius is unique in stating that the ceremony of *sexagenarii de ponte* took place on the Milvian rather than the Sublician Bridge. Editors have contemplated emendation

---

[7] *Rh. Mus.* 79 (1930), 279–302.
[8] *Aetna* (Cambridge, 1965), 102.

(*Aemilio* Jordan; *Sublicio* Brandt). But the explanation is simple. There is no evidence that Lactantius knew Rome, but he would have known of the battle of the Milvian Bridge in A.D. 312.

In classical times several works passed under the authorship of 'Orpheus'—some of them went back to the sixth century but the date and origin of most of them is uncertain. They were increasingly fashionable under the Empire and were widely used both by Christians and Neo-Platonists. The two most popular were the Ἱεροὶ Λόγοι in twenty-four books, basically a Theogony in content, and the Διαθῆκαι, a Last Will and Testament in which 'Orpheus' retracted his belief in polytheism. A *terminus ante quem* for both is given by their citation in Athenagoras and Clement of Alexandria. Lactantius knew of both works but the sole reference to the Διαθῆκαι, mentioning the fact that 'Orpheus' postulated 365 gods (*D.I.* 1.7.7), was a commonplace, one in any case quoted by Theophilus (*Ad Autol.* 3.2)—a work known to have been extensively used by Lactantius. The citations from the Ἱεροὶ Λόγοι are a different matter. Four of the five quotations concern Phanes and the creation of the universe. The first (73 K. = 1.5.5) is odd. According to Lactantius, Phanes was born from air (*ex aere*) because there was nothing else conceivable that he could be born from. He then quotes

πρωτόγονος φαέθων περιμήκεος ἠέρος υἱός.[9]

πρωτόγονος was the standard epithet (cf. *D.I.* 1.5.13–14; *Epit.* 3) and φαέθων must be a participle, not the name Phaethon, but Proclus, who also seems to be utilizing the same passage (*in Plat. Tim.* 31 a), calls Phanes περικάλλεος Αἰθέρος υἱός (= fr. 74 K.; cf. fr. 75 K. = *Etym. M.* 787, 29 Φάνητα ὅτι πρῶτος ἐν αἰθέρι φάντος ἐγένετο).

The reading ἠέρος in Lactantius is not wholly certain but is confirmed in my view by the preceding Latin words *ex aere*. If Lactantius and Proclus do refer to the same line, only a divergence of traditions or a failure of memory will account for the variants περιμήκεος ἠέρος and περικάλλεος αἰθέρος. The third is a passing reference in Latin to the bisexual nature of Phanes (4.8.4) which is given in the original Greek by Proclus (*in Plat.*

[9] [ΗΕ]ΡΩΣ B: ΙΕΡΟC R: Αἰθέρος Kern.

*Tim.* 30 c-d = fr. 81 K.). The fourth (89 K. = *D.I.* 1.5.6) follows on the first and states that Phanes built a home for the gods that he had created: ἔκτισεν ἀθανάτοις δόμον ἄφθιτον. This half-line is not known from any source, nor does any other writer mention the fact, although it is implicit in the account of Phanes' cosmogonical activities. The fifth and final quotation is a couplet describing Cronos' original reign over men and his succession by his son, Zeus (fr. 139 K. = 1.13.11). This will have occurred soon after the Phanes passage, and the gist of it is known from many other fragments (cf. 128 K.). The 'Orphic' tradition on the question goes back at least to the time of Plato's *Cratylus*.

Unlike Musaeus, the Orphic Ἱεροὶ Λόγοι or, to be precise, a very short section from one of the twenty-four books, seems to have been known by Lactantius, either at first hand or from some Neo-Platonist writer (cf. *Op.* 8.10). And this is not surprising, given its wide appeal at the time. In that respect it resembles the other primary work of Greek poetry quoted by him, the *Oracula Sibyllina*.

# III.   Sibylline and Hermetic Writings

ONE of Lactantius' most original weapons was his use of the *Oracula Sibyllina* and various Hermetic tracts as evidence, from the pagan side, of the truth of Christianity. He believed that these collections of writings were of great antiquity, certainly pre-Christian (4.15.26). In this belief he was naïve and wrong. Nevertheless his use of this material was a major contribution to Christian apologetics, especially in the West, and is of great interest on its own account.

The Sibylline Oracles, as they have been preserved in our manuscripts, represent a heterogeneous anthology. The core of the extant twelve hexameter-poems (there were originally at least fourteen) comprises 3, 4, and 5, which were probably composed in a Judaeo-Hellenistic community in the Early Empire. Their thought has much in common with that of Philo, and the allusions only have point if they refer to relatively recent events (e.g. 3.51–2 The Second Triumvirate, 3.357 Cleopatra, 4.119–20 Nero). The other poems were written much later, as the fact that Lactantius knows only 3, 4, 5, 6, possibly 7, and 8 proves.[1]

They had been utilized earlier in Christian apologetic by such writers as Athenagoras, Tertullian, and Clement of Alexandria, and above all by Theophilus of Antioch in his work *Ad Autolycum* (p. 92).[2] The *Ad Autolycum* with its easy, informal style, was a popular work, which Lactantius knew well. He names it explicitly once (1.23.2) and paraphrases it unmistakably elsewhere (4.5.6–8). It is also clear that some of his quotations of the Sibylline Oracles come directly from Theophilus, even if Theophilus may not, himself either, have quoted from the text of the Oracles at first hand. The crucial

[1] A. Rzach, *Oracula Sibyllina* (Vienna, 1891); J. Geffcken, *Die Oracula Sibyllina* (Leipzig, 1902). The earliest evidence for the Oracles comes from Antisthenes of Rhodes (*c.* 150 B.C.: see A. Momigliano, *Alien Wisdom*, 40).

For Lactantius and the Sibylline Oracles see, recently, A. Kurfess, *Th.Q.* 131 (1951), 458; 133 (1953), 90; Dornseiff, *Röm. Lit. d. aug. Zeit* (1961), 43–51.

[2] *Theophilus of Antioch*, ed. R. M. Grant (Oxford, 1971).

text is 4.6.5: Sibylla Erythraea in carminis sui principio, quod a summo deo exorsa est, filium dei ducem et imperatorem omnium his versibus praedicat

παντοτρόφον κτίστην, ὅστις γλυκὺ πνεῦμα ἄπασιν
κάτθετο χἠγητῆρα θεὸν πάντων ἐποίησεν.

The 'Erythraean Sibyl' was the authoress of *O.S.* 3 according to the unanimous tradition of antiquity, and Lactantius continues by quoting a final line ('in fine'), ἄλλον ἔδωκε θεὸς πιστοῖς ἄνδρεσσι γεραίρειν which is line 774 of *O.S.* 3. Now our manuscript texts of *O.S.* 3 continue to line 829 and do not contain the opening lines which Lactantius quotes. Although line 774, out of a total of 829, could perhaps be called 'in fine', it is certain that Lactantius owes the opening lines to Theophilus (2.36) who gives an extended quotation (fr. 1 Geffcken) which he claims occurred ἐν ἀρχῇ τῆς προφητείας of the Erythraean Sibyl. It follows that in the second to fourth centuries A.D. what we know as *O.S.* 3 was prefaced by the long passage which Theophilus preserves, and that, therefore, Theophilus and Lactantius are primary sources for the early state of the Sibylline texts. This is readily confirmed by Geffcken's detailed comparison of Lactantius' citations with the versions handed down in our manuscripts. Wherever there is a difference, it can be asserted that Lactantius preserves an older, purer tradition.

Geffcken, following Rzach, classified the manuscripts of the *O.S.* into three branches *ΩΦΨ*. The following passages illustrate the state of the text:

| | | |
|---|---|---|
| 4.43 | ἐν πυρί Lact.: | ἔμπαλιν *ΩΦΨ* |
| 6.15 | πήρης Lact.: | σπείρης *Ω*: ῥίζης *ΦΨ* |
| 4.52 | πολίεσσι Lact.: | πόλεσσι *Ω*: πόλεσίν τε *ΦΨ* |
| 8.260 | θεοῦ παλάμαις ἁγίαισιν Lact.: | θεοῦ παλάμῃσιν *Ω*: om. *ΦΨ* |
| 4.42 | ἀσεβεῖς θ' ἅμα Lact.: | ἀσεβεῖς ἅμα τ' *ΩΦΨ* |

But the passage at 4.6.5 is more complicated. In the first place, although Lactantius seems to have derived the opening lines from Theophilus, the additional line (*O.S.* 3.774) was not quoted by Theophilus and therefore was supplied by Lactantius from his own knowledge. Secondly, even the lines that he does quote from Theophilus do not agree exactly with the text of Theophilus that has been transmitted to us, as the following Apparatus shows:

πνεῦμ' ἐν ἅπασιν Theoph.: πνεῦμα ἅπασιν RHSP
θεὸν B: ΘΝ SP: θεῶν RV: βροτῶν Theoph.

This same phenomenon is apparent in the other quotations which can plausibly be attributed to Theophilus as the prime intermediary. Thus, Lactantius quotes from the same opening of *O.S.* 3 ( =fr. 1 Geffcken) elsewhere in *D.I.* 1.6.15–16

εἷς θεός, ὃς μόνος ἄρχει, ὑπερμεγέθης ἀγένητος

and

αὐτὸν τὸν μόνον ὄντα σέβεσθ' ἡγήτορα κόσμου
ὃς μόνος εἰς αἰῶνα καὶ ἐξ αἰῶνος ἐτύχθη

but Theophilus' text reads θεὸς[ὃς]μόνος (cf. Aesch. *P.V.* 354). Theophilus has a second long fragment which is not found in the manuscripts of the *Oracula Sibyllina* (*Ad Autol.* 2.36 = fr.3 Geffcken). Lactantius quotes some lines from this fragment also, but again with some divergences from Theophilus' text.

1.6.15    ἀλλὰ θεὸς μόνος [*om.* Theoph.] εἷς πανυπέρτατος ὃς
          πεποίηκεν
          . . . ὕδατος οἴδματα [οἶδμα Theoph.] πόντου

2.12.19   ζωὴν κληρονομοῦσι [κληρονομήσουσιν Theoph.] τὸν αἰῶνος
          χρόνον αὐτοί
          οἰκοῦντες Παράδεισον ὁμῶς [*om.* Theoph.], ἐριθήλεα κῆπον.

(It is to be noted that this last passage comes after a clear paraphrase of Theophilus, *Ad Autol.* 103 A.)

The solution to this last problem is relatively easy. The manuscript tradition of Lactantius is early and good,[3] whereas the tradition of Theophilus depends upon a single Venetian manuscript of the tenth century. Since in all cases where there are variants, Lactantius preserves a better text, it can be inferred that he knew an older and less corrupt version of Theophilus' text. The first problem remains, but it can be shown that Lactantius knew the Sibylline Oracles quite independently of the lines which he borrowed from Theophilus, so that it should be no surprise if he elaborates on a text which he is using. He does the same thing elsewhere. At 4.6.5

---

[3] But he may have made changes between the first and second editions; cf. e.g. *D.I.*4.19.10 (= *O.S.* 8.314) θνητοῖς B: κλητοῖς RSP.

and 1.6.16 he quotes passages from the Eighth Sibylline Oracle (8.329, 8.377). On both occasions he has just quoted from Theophilus but the passages from Book 8 do not appear in Theophilus and, moreover, they are each introduced by the significant word *alia* (1.6.16 'item alia Sibylla quaecumque est . . . sic ait'; 4.6.5 'et alia Sibylla praecipit'), which implies that Lactantius is consciously adding something of his own. Now we know that he was familiar with the opening of *O.S.* 8 ( = *De Ira* 23.3 'hoc modo exorsa est') and that, therefore, this poem, which is quoted more than thirty-five times, was part of his basic raw material.

Lactantius makes use of the Sibylline Oracles in two main ways. In Book 7 he paraphrases them extensively to give an apocalyptic view of the future of the world. Actual references are also frequent (7.15.18 'Sibyllae tamen aperte interituram esse Romam locuntur . . .' = 8.9 ff.; 7.16.11 σάλπιγξ . . . ἀφήσει = 8.239; 7.16.13 'in carminibus Sibyllinis ita dicitur ἔσται κόσμος ἄκοσμος . . .' = 7.123; 7.18.6 = 5.107–9; 7.18.7 = 3.652–3; 7.18.8 = 8.326–8; 7.19.9 = 8.224, 3.618; 7.20.2 = 3.741–3; 7.20.3 = 8.241–2; 7.20.4 = 8.413–16; 7.23.4 = 4.40–3, 186–7; 7.24.1 = 8.81–3; 7.24.2 = fr.4 Geffcken; 7.24.6 = 5.420–1; 7.24.12 = 3.787–91; 7.24.13 = 3.619–23; 7.24.14 = 5.281–3) and their effect is cumulatively impressive.

Secondly in Book 4 he illustrates biblical texts with carefully chosen extracts from the Sibylline Oracles. We are fortunate to have Augustine's independent evidence about Lactantius' method of composition which makes it certain that, wherever he may have got his biblical quotations from, he was personally responsible for the Sibylline parallels: 'inserit autem Lactantius operi suo quaedam de Christo ratiocinia Sibyllae, quamvis non exprimit cuius. Sed quae ipse singillatim posuit, ego arbitratus sum coniuncta esse ponenda . . . Lactantius carptim per intervalla disputationis suae, sicut ea poscere videbantur quae probare intenderat, adhibuit testimonia Sibyllina' (*C.D.* 18.23: he then proceeds to translate *O.S.* 8.287 ff., quoted by Lactantius 4.18.15). These extensive quotations are confined to chapters 13–20 of Book 4 and are mainly derived from *O.S.* 3, 6, and 8. They constitute one of Lactantius' most forceful contributions to the evangelical cause.[4]

[4] Pichon, *Lactance*, 207 ff.

Outside these two main sections Lactantius alludes only rarely to the Oracles. This corroborates a more general view about his manner of work, namely that he tended to have a particular book on hand when he was working on a particular topic, and would then disregard it for long stretches. But there still remain a number of unresolved issues. Lactantius, it has been argued, derived some of his quotations of the Sibyl from Theophilus and some from first-hand acquaintance with an early text of the Oracles themselves. There are, however, a few passages which have no counterpart either in Theophilus or in the manuscripts of the *O.S.* In particular *D.I.* 7.24.2 quod alia Sibylla vaticinans . . . proclamat:

$$κλῦτε\ δέ\ μου,\ μέροπες,\ βασιλεὺς\ αἰώνιος\ ἄρχει.$$

2.11.18    Sibylla hominem dei opus esse testatur:

$$ὃς\ μόνος\ ἐστὶ\ θεὸς\ κτίστης\ ἀκράτητος\ ὑπάρχων$$
$$αὐτὸς\ δ'\ ἐστήριξε\ τύπον\ μορφῆς\ μερόπων\ τε,$$
$$αὐτὸς\ ἔμιξε\ φύσιν\ πάντων,\ γενέτης\ βιότοιο$$

and 7.19.2 $ὁππόταν\ ἔλθῃ\ |\ πῦρ\ ἔσται\ σκοτόεν\ τι\ μέσῃ\ ἐνὶ\ νυκτὶ\ μελαίνῃ.$[5]

One can only assume that Lactantius found these lines in his collection of the *O.S.* but they were subsequently lost or not transmitted through the manuscript tradition.[6] He himself draws attention to the confused and corrupt state of the texts that were circulating in his day (*D.I.* 1.6.13; cf. *de Ira* 23). The same conclusion should probably be drawn about 5.13.21 'quos Sibylla Erythraea $κωφοὺς$ et $ἀνοήτους$ vocat'. This should come from *O.S.* 3 but the words are not found in the surviving poem and the parallel from *O.S.* 8.397 $κωφοὺς\ καὶ\ ἀναύδεις$ is irrelevant, since Lactantius certainly was thinking of 'senseless' (he translates 'surdos et excordes'). However, *O.S.* 3 was substantially different then from the form in which we now have it and this phrase must have occurred in it.

A final difficulty is raised by fr.1 (Geffcken). Lactantius quoted line 7 $εἷς\ θεὸς\ ὃς\ μόνος\ ἄρχει\ ὑπερμεγέθης\ ἀγένητος$ and lines 15–16 $αὐτὸν\ τὸν\ μόνον\ .\ .\ .\ ἐτύχθη$ which are followed in Theophilus by the line $αὐτογενὴς\ ἀγένητος\ ἄπαντα\ κρατῶν\ διάπαντος$ but not in Lactantius (*D.I.* 1.6.15–16). Yet when he

---

[5] $σκοτόεν\ τι$ Struve: $σκτοεν$ B: $σκότος$ Sedulius: $ψολόεν$ Stadtmüller.

[6] None of the manuscripts of the oracles, which fall into three classes, is earlier than the fifteenth century.

resumes the argument at 1.7.13, referring back to his earlier quotations of the Sibyl and of Apollo, he writes: 'a Sibylla αὐτογενής et ἀγένητος et ἀποίητος nominatur'. Now either the line αὐτογενής . . . διάπαντος has dropped out from the manuscripts at 1.6.16 or else Lactantius is quoting carelessly from memory, forgetting that he had not actually cited the line in question. The former is the more likely possibility, since he explicitly repeats Apollo's αὐτοφυής from 1.7.1. Even so ἀποίητος leaves a problem. It does not figure anywhere in fr.1, and is not commonly used in patristic or philosophical Greek for 'uncreated'. With Struve,[7] I think 'et ἀποίητος' must be deleted as a gloss. Its removal also helps the syntax, eliminating a very unusual instance of A *et* B *et* C in Lactantius.

A literary phenomenon not unlike the Sibylline Oracles was the growth of Hermetic writing under the early Empire.[8] This consisted of Discourses, written by Greek-speaking Egyptians on philosophical and religious themes with a strong apocalyptic flavour. They purported to have been composed by the god Thoth or Hermes the Very Great (Trismegistos) to various pupils such as Tat, Asclepius, or Ammon, and to convey the essential knowledge or *gnosis* about the Universe. Although Hermes was supposed to have lived in high antiquity (before the sixth century B.C.), in fact the discourses date chiefly from the second and third centuries A.D. Surprisingly they contain little that is distinctively Egyptian, Judaic, or Christian in character but reflect rather the mystical contents of Neo-Platonism. Their ascription to Hermes was designed to give them authority and respectability. The first Christian to make use of them was Athenagoras (*c*. A.D. 180) who was followed by Tertullian and the author of the *Cohortatio ad gentes* (*c*. A.D. 280); the first pagan to allude to them was Porphyry but he, like Clement and Origen, largely ignored them, presumably because he was aware that they were not authentic documents of great age.

Three groups of Hermetic writings have survived from classical times. The first is a collection of some eighteen pieces, preserved in fourteenth-century manuscripts and known as the Corpus Hermeticum, which was probably formed or at least

---

[7] *Opuscula Selecta*, 1.54.
[8] W. Scott and A. S. Ferguson, *Hermetica* (1924–36); A. D. Nock and A. J. Festugière, *Corpus Hermeticum* (Paris, 1945–54).

edited by Michael Psellus *c.* A.D. 1050. The second is a Latin translation of the three books of the dialogue *Asclepius*. The Greek original, called the Λόγος Τέλειος (*Perfectus Sermo*; cf. 6.25.11, 4.6.4), was probably written about A.D. 270 and the Latin translation, which has come down to us under the name of Apuleius, was almost certainly made after A.D. 353 and before about 420 (it is utilized by Augustine in the *De Civitate Dei*). Lactantius knew the Greek but not the Latin version. Thirdly Stobaeus (*c.* A.D. 500) included a large number of excerpts in his Anthology: some of these correspond to passages of the 'Asclepius' or of the discourses in the C.H. but some are not otherwise known. This shows that in Lactantius' day, and for several centuries thereafter, there were several Hermetic works in circulation which have now disappeared.

Lactantius himself knew the complete Λόγος Τέλειος from which he takes four quotations in Greek and one in Latin. The Greek quotations are important because they enable us to restore passages which are only inaccurately transmitted in the poor Latin 'Asclepius'. For instance the long sentence at *D.I.* 7.18.4 (=Asclep.26) contains three important readings ('τοῦ πρώτου καὶ ἑνὸς θεοῦ ~ deus, primi[potens] et unius gubernator dei'; ἐκκαθάρας, omitted by Asclepius; πολέμοις καὶ for which Asclepius substitutes 'dispersis', apparently having a reading such as πολυσπέρεσι). On the other hand, at 4.6.4 it is the turn of Lactantius' Greek to be corrected in the light of Asclepius 8 (e.g. the supplement ἢ μή, εἰσαῦθις ῥηθήσεται = 'an non, alio dicemus tempore'; καὶ εἰς ὅρασιν ~ 'videntium sensus'). At 6.25.11 he offers a Latin translation of his own which affords an instructive contrast with the poor style of 'Asclepius' (*Epil.* 41a). To Asclepius' question whether incense is pleasing to god, he replies: 'Bene, bene ominare, o Asclepi; est enim maxima inpietas tale quid de uno illo ac singulari bono in animum inducere. haec et his similia huic non conveniunt: omnium enim quaecumque sunt plenus est et omnium minime indigens. nos vero gratias agentes adoremus: huius enim sacrificium sola benedictio est.' In the later version the reply is: 'Melius, melius ominare, Asclepi: hoc enim sacrilegii simile est, cum deum roges, tus ceteraque incendere. Nihil enim deest ei qui ipse est omnia aut in eo sunt òmnia. Sed nos agentes gratias adoremus: hae sunt enim summi (*Scott:* summae *codd.*) incensiones dei, gratiae cum aguntur a mortalibus.' The clumsy addition of 'in eo sunt omnia', the inelegant 'cum . . . roges', and the late 'incensiones' all betray the hand of the amateur while the solemn *o*, the Ciceronian 'in animum inducere', the rhetorical 'haec et his similia', 'omnium . . . omnium' are deliberately and stylistically written. At times the two versions are widely divergent, and one must assume that 'Asclepius' has made a fairly free paraphrase (cf. e.g. 7.13.3 ~ Asclep. 8: but note θαυμάζῃ–'mirari'). Lactantius set great store by the Λόγος Τέλειος and drew widely on it, as on the Sibylline Oracles, for his general eschatology in 7.14. In view of this dependence, it is strange that he should appear at 2.15.6 to confuse it with another Hermetic work. There he uses 'perfectus sermo' as the Latin title of a letter written by Asclepius to the king, which, in fact, is Corpus Hermeticum 16, Asclepius to Ammon. The mistake probably arose from a lapse of memory, occasioned by the fact that C.H.16 opens with the claim that it is the summing up (κορυφή) of all Hermetic teaching.

In addition to C.H.16 Lactantius quotes from 1 (2.10.14), 5 (1.6.4, 2.19.14), 9 (2.15.6, 5.14.11), 10 (1.11.61, 3.30.3) and 12 (6.25.10). The quotations or translations are often little more than free adaptations and may have been tampered with by Lactantius himself (e.g. the addition of Mercury at 1.11.61), but we do not know how far the texts of the C.H. themselves may have been distorted in the course of transmission. Lactantius' wide reading in the Hermetica is further evidenced by the fact that another two quotations, including the very important one on the four elements (2.12.4, 7.9.11), recur in Stobaeus' selection (*Excerpts* II a 6; II a 2) and a third (2.8.68) is also employed by Cyril of Alexandria (*c.* A.D. 440) in his *Against Julian* (p. 31C Aub.). But his reading widened with time and opportunities. This, therefore, may account for the fact that he only quotes the famous θεὸν νοῆσαι μέν ἐστι χαλεπόν κτλ. (Stobaeus, *Excerpts* I; also in Cyril, *Against Julian* 31; Ps. Justin, *Cohortatio ad Gent.*38) in the *Epitome* (4.5) and not in the *D.I.* itself, though he may have come across it orally and not in a written text, for he certainly knew it as θεὸν μὲν νοῆσαι (='deum quidem intellegere') not θεὸν νοῆσαι μέν and he renders τὸ ἀσώματον σώματι by the inexact 'invisibile a visibili'. A few further passages (4.7.3, 1.7.2, 4.8.5, 4.13.2) are nowhere else attested but this is only further evidence of the quantity of Hermetic tracts in circulation.

Lactantius had an almost blind faith in Hermes Trismegistos —'homo antiquissimus et instructissimus omni genere doctrinae', as he called him (1.5.3). He did not inquire into the origins, sources, or date of the writings attributed to Hermes but assumed that they were authentic prophecies and, therefore, parallel to biblical prophecies (6.25.10 'idoneus testis est qui nobiscum, id est cum prophetis quos sequimur, tam re quam verbis congruit'). In so far as what Hermes had to say on God, human nature, demons, and the destruction and recreation of the world agreed closely with Lactantius' own beliefs, he was glad to welcome him as a powerful ally. If such an approach seems to us to be uncritical and unhistorical, it was characteristic of Lactantius' age. The fascination that Hermetic writings had for his generation is revealed in the frequent appeals which both sides made to them in the Arian controversy and to the great popularity of debased Hermetism in magical and superstitious circles.

# IV.   Historians and Antiquarians

LACTANTIUS' use of Greek and Roman poets is relatively easy to control and yields some revealing conclusions. It is inevitably harder to analyse in depth his knowledge of classical prose-writers. Quotations can be more readily corrupted, misattributed, or taken over at second hand. This chapter is concerned with his knowledge of Greek and Roman historians or writers on general antiquarian subjects.

The most striking feature is the absence of any reference to Herodotus, Thucydides, or Polybius, authors who continued to command great interest and attention under the Empire. Plutarch is not mentioned by name but two passages have been cited in the belief that Lactantius knew him, as he might conceivably have done since Plutarch had such an influence on the development of neo-Platonism. On closer examination, however, neither passage demands first-hand acquaintance. In *D.I.* 3.19.17 he quotes a saying of Plato's about his good fortune in being born a man, a male, a Greek, an Athenian, and a contemporary of Socrates. The same remark is also quoted by Plutarch in his *Life* of Marius (46) but it was obviously a traditional saying like many others ascribed to Plato. In *De Ira* 13.10–12 a commonplace about the usefulness of mice is also reflected in Plutarch's *Stoic. Repugn.* 21.4. It will have been a τόπος used in philosophical arguments.

Four other Greek historians are named—Apollodorus of Erythrae, Heraclides Ponticus, Eratosthenes, and Nicanor—but all in the long section on the various Sibyls, which is from Varro's *Libri Rerum Divinarum* (1.6.7–12). It cannot be suggested that Lactantius went any further than the pages of Varro, if as far as that.

A more complex issue is involved in his quotation of Diodorus Siculus and Thallus. In an elaborate argument designed to show that even classical scholars thought that Saturn really was a man, he writes as follows: 'omnes ergo non tantum poetae, sed historiarum quoque ac rerum antiquarum scriptores hominem fuisse consentiunt, qui res eius in Italia gestas memoriae prodiderunt, Graeci Diodorus et Thallus, Latini Nepos et Cassius et Varro' (*D.I.* 1.13.8). But the whole of that sentence is simply taken from Minucius Felix, with the significant addition of Varro: 'Saturnum enim, principem huius generis et examinis, omnes scriptores vetustatis Graeci Romanique hominem tradiderunt. Scit hoc Nepos et Cassius in historia, et Thallus ac Diodorus hoc loquuntur' (*Oct.* 21.4).

Neither Diodorus nor Cassius Hemina is quoted elsewhere. Thallus surprisingly is, at 1.23.2, but there again the context makes it clear that the allusion is made at second hand, this time from Theophilus, *Ad Autolycum* (see p. 92): 'Theophilus in libro ad Autolycum scripto ait in historia sua Thallum dicere quod Belus . . . antiquior Troiano bello fuisse inveniatur' (=3.29). Nepos is considered below.

That, then, is the sum total of Lactantius' Greek antiquarianism. He had not, so far as we can tell, read anyone in the original.

The Latin story is naturally more complex. Leaving aside for the moment his debt to Ennius' Euhemerus, Cicero, and Varro, we can eliminate a number of writers whom Brandt and others have tried to detect. Cassius Hemina, the annalist, has already been accounted for. Nepos is also cited in 3.5.10 where a letter of his to Cicero is used to illustrate the failure of philosophers to live up to their philosophy. Now Nepos did correspond with his friend Cicero (*ad Att.* 16.5.5) and a collection of his correspondence is presumed by Suetonius (*Jul.* 55.2, quoting a letter of Cicero to Nepos on Caesar's oratory) and by Macrobius (*Sat.* 2.1.14, quoting a letter from the second volume of Cicero's correspondence to Nepos), but the collection is not known elsewhere and the context in Lactantius, with its rhetorical overtones, suggests that the comment comes from Seneca's *Exhortationes* and not from personal reading. Something similar will be true of the story of Cimon's philanthropy (6.9.8)—an *exemplum* told by Nepos (*Cimon* 4) but which Lactantius does not specifically attribute to him and which Mai and other scholars agree in thinking was in fact derived from a missing portion of the third book of Cicero's *De Rep.*, a work widely employed here and elsewhere in the *D.I.*

Scholars have also tried to detect the influence of Florus but

Lactantius never refers to him by name and of the four passages put forward, two (1.15.32, 1.22.1–4) are certainly based on Livy, a third (7.15.14) is explicitly claimed for Seneca[1] (a claim not to be explained away by a confusion between Annaeus Seneca and Annius Florus), and the fourth (5.13.13, the *exempla* of Mucius Scaevola and Regulus) is a commonplace also utilized by Minucius Felix 37.3 and could have come from Minucius, Valerius Maximus, or any handbook of *exempla*.

Varro must be the ultimate source for some other quotations. He is, explicitly, for the solitary mention of the annalist Piso (1.6.8—the list of Sibyls) and, most probably, as E. Schwartz argued,[2] of Tarquitius, *De Viris Illustribus* (1.10.1). One passage (1.22.9–12), dealing with divergent stories about Faunus, is particularly relevant.

sed ut Pompilius aput Romanos institutor ineptarum religionum fuit, sic ante Pompilium Faunus in Latio, qui et Saturno auo nefaria sacra constituit et Picum patrem inter deos honorauit et sororem suam Fentam Faunam eandemque coniugem consecrauit; quam Gauius Bassus tradit Fatuam nominatam, quod mulieribus fata canere consuesset ut Faunus uiris. eandem Varro scribit tantae pudicitiae fuisse, ut nemo illam quoad uixerit praeter suum uirum mas uiderit nec nomen eius audierit. idcirco illi mulieres in operto sacrificant et Bonam Deam nominant. et Sextus Clodius in eo libro quem graece scripsit, refert Fauni hanc uxorem fuisse; quae quia contra morem decusque regium clam uini ollam ebiberat et ebria facta erat, uirgis myrteis a uiro ad mortem usque caesam; postea uero cum eum facti sui paeniteret ac desiderium eius ferre non posset, diuinum illi honorem detulisse; idcirco in sacris eius obuolutam uini amphoram poni. reliquit ergo posteris Faunus quoque non parum erroris, quem tamen prudentes quique perspiciunt.

Gavius Bassus was a contemporary of Cicero's. He wrote one work (*De Origine Verborum*) which is cited several times by Aulus Gellius. It became part of traditional grammatical material. Another work—*De Diis*—is mentioned in passing by Macrobius, for the history of Janus. It is from this work that the Faunus discussion presumably comes. Sextus Clodius is less

[1] We need no longer consider the possibility that the Seneca in question is the elder Seneca, who is credited with a History, perhaps never published (M. T. Griffin, *J.R.S.* 62 (1972), 14 with bibliography). The fragment comes from one of the younger Seneca's philosophical works.

[2] *Annal. Phil.* Suppl. 16 (1888), 420.

certainly identifiable but he can hardly be other than the famous Sicilian rhetorician (Suet. *Gramm.* 29) who was the teacher of M. Antonius, the Triumvir. Arnobius (*Adv. Nat.* 5.18) also gives an account of Clodius' discussion of Fatua (from the sixth book in Greek *De Diis*), which is very similar to but fuller than Lactantius'. Both Gavius and Clodius were active in the life-time of Varro and it is Varro whose name links the two together. It is possible therefore that Varro quoted both in his discussion and that Lactantius has got the references from Varro but it is equally possible that all three accounts were already in the collection of apologetic material used by Arnobius.

There is much less certainty about Fenestella, not least because there is so little certain evidence about him. The authorities date him from 52 B.C. to A.D. 19 (Jerome *anno* 2035) although Wissowa[3] has argued, on the basis of Pliny (*N.H.* 33.146 'novissimo Tiberii principatu') for a later date of 35 B.C. to A.D. 36. Whatever the true dates he must have been later than Varro, and, significantly, he is listed third by Asconius (Cic. *Corn.* p. 53 St.) after Sallust and Livy.

The sources are not unanimous. Lydus (*De Mag.* 3.74) states that Varro used Fenestella and Sisenna, although he admits that he has not yet seen the actual books (ὡς Φενέστελλας καὶ Σισέννας οἱ ʿΡωμαῖοί φασιν ὧν τὰς χρήσεις ὁ Βάρρων ἐπὶ τῶν ἀνθρωπίνων πραγμάτων ἀνήγαγεν. ἐγὼ δὲ τὰς βίβλους οὔπω τεθέαμμαι). Varro's *Human Antiquities* was published in 47 B.C. Furthermore Lactantius links the names of Fenestella and Varro in *De Ira* 22.5, and in *D.I.* 1.6.14 quotes him for the story of how the *carmina* of the Erythraean Sibyl were brought to Rome—a subject treated by Varro. Nevertheless it is difficult to believe that Varro could have used Fenestella, not least because Fenestella is on record as saying thàt he had seen and talked with an old woman who, as a girl, had looked after Crassus in a cave during the late 80s B.C. Fenestella was a popular writer: he was much used by the elder Pliny and was known to Tertullian (*Adv. Val.* 34).

As for Pescennius Festus, who is quoted on Carthaginian human sacrifice (1.21.13), he is unknown elsewhere. A Pescennius Festus, alleged to have been killed by Septimius

---

[3] Wissowa, *R.E.*, 'Fenestella', coll. 2177 ff.

Severus, is, along with others in that list, a fiction (*S.H.A. Sept. Sev.* 13.6).[4] Nothing can be said about him.

We are on firmer ground with the major historians. Sallust's monographs and histories were widely read down to late antiquity. Papyri of all three works have been found at Oxyrhyncus, but Lactantius was probably only acquainted with the *Catiline*, and the more philosophical parts of it at that. He does indeed refer to some phrases from the *Histories* but the nature of the phrases indicates their immediate source. Appius' saying *canina facundia* (6.18.26 'sic ut Sallustius refert' = fr. 4.54 M.) was proverbial (cf. Quint. 12.9.9; Jerome, *Epist.* 119.1, 125.16, 134.1). The words *venditis aut dilargitis*, unattributed by Lactantius (7.1.13), come ultimately from *Hist.* 1.49.19 M. but were famous as a grammatical example of the passive use of *dilargitis* (Aul. Gell. 15.13.8; Priscian 8.392 K.). At 1.21.41 he is cited for a theory about the Curetes, who, he believes, were not the guards or nurses of Juppiter but the first people to understand religion: 'hanc totam opinionem quasi a poetis fictam Sallustius respuit uoluitque ingeniose interpretari, cur altores Iouis dicantur fuisse Curetes, et sic ait, quia principes diuini intellegendi fuerunt, uetustatem ut cetera in maius componentem altores Iouis celebrauisse'. We have already seen that the birth of Juppiter was a popular *quaestio*, discussed, for instance, by the commentators on the *Aratea* (above, p. 13). That Sallust's view formed part of this traditional stock of opinion is clear from Servius, *Ad Aen.* 3.104: 'illic dicitur esse nutritus, quod, ut Sallustius dicit, ideo fingitur quia primos Cretenses constat invenisse religionem'.[5] There is only one allusion claimed for the *Jugurtha* (4.16.3 ~ *Jug.* 1.3) but that is too remote to merit further examination. But the *Catiline* he certainly knew. He quotes some opening sentences (1.2) at *D.I.* 2.12.12 and refers to them again at 6.1.7. They were, it is true, famous and are also quoted by Servius, Jerome and Fulgentius, but in addition there is an extensive quotation from *Cat.* 8.1 on fortune (*D.I.* 3.29.8,10). I doubt whether anything can be inferred from the common use of *extruere mare* (*Cat.* 20.11 ~ *D.I.* 7.3.9) or from the very free paraphrases of *Cat.* 10 and

---

[4] Syme, *Ammianus and Historia Augusta*, 155 n. 2.
[5] Cf. also Epit. 54.7 'ius in viribus' with *Hist.* 1.18 M.—again proverbial, 'Might is right'.

12.2 at *D.I.* 7.15.15 and 6.1.8, which may well come at second hand from authors such as Seneca.

The first book of Livy enjoyed great popularity. It is significant that the sole papyrus fragment of Livy comes from that book, that Claudian appears only to have known the first decade and primarily imitates passages from the first book, that the earliest surviving manuscript was of that decade and that Symmachus limited his editorial interest to the same books. Livy is in fact only quoted once by name (1.20.2) on the story of Larentina (Livy 1.4.8) but three other passages are certainly due to him, on the asylum (2.6.13 = Livy 1.8), on the apotheosis of Romulus (1.15.32 = Livy 1.7.9: note the phrase 'humano habitu augustiorem') and on Numa (1.22.1–4). This last passage has some very close linguistic resemblances to the corresponding passage of Livy:

Harum vanitatum aput Romanos auctor et constitutor Sabinus ille rex fuit, qui maxime animos hominum rudes atque inperitos novis superstitionibus implicavit: quod ut faceret aliqua cum auctoritate, simulavit cum dea Egeria nocturnos se habere congressus. erat spelunca quaedam peropaca in nemore Aricino, unde rivus perenni fonte manabat. huc se remotis arbitris inferre consueverat, ut mentiri posset monitu deae coniugis ea sacra populo se tradere, quae acceptissima diis essent. videlicet astutiam Minois voluit imitari, qui se in antrum Iovis recondebat et ibi diu moratus leges tamquam sibi a Iove traditas adferebat, ut homines ad parendum non modo imperio, sed etiam religione constringeret. nec difficile sane fuit persuadere pastoribus. itaque pontifices flamines Salios augures creavit, deos per familias discripsit: sic novi populi feroces animos mitigavit et ad studia pacis a rebus bellicis avocavit.

Quibus cum inter bella adsuescere videret non posse, quippe efferari militia animos, mitigandum ferocem populum armorum desuetudine ratus . . . (Livy 1.19.2).

Qui cum descendere ad animos sine aliquo commento miraculi non posset, simulat sibi cum dea Egeria congressus nocturnos esse; eius se monitu, quae acceptissima diis essent sacra instituere, sacerdotes suos cuique deorum praeficere (1.19.5).

Lucus erat, quem medium ex opaco specu fons perenni rigabat aqua. Quo quia se persaepe Numa sine arbitris velut ad congressum deae inferebat, Camenis eum lucum sacravit, quod earum ibi concilia cum coniuge sua Egeria essent; et Fidei sollemne instituit (1.21.3).

But that is the extent of the debt: other historical illustrations would appear to come from more manageable sources.

Tacitus he did not know and does not refer to. Brandt claimed a reminiscence of *Germania* 40 on *D.I.* 1.11.12 ('illud quod tantum perituri vident'). It is, however, a common epigram that needs no such recondite source.

There had been a long tradition among Christian writers of citing *exempla* from classical history to illustrate or confute propositions. In this they were, of course, doing no more than following the practice of the rhetorical schools, a practice which is often prescribed by Cicero and which can be seen extensively in the works of poets like Juvenal. What is interesting is that Tertullian, Minucius Felix, and Lactantius use pagan *exempla* and only very rarely biblical ones. That is in line with their general policy of making Christianity acceptable to an educated Roman world.[6]

Some of the *exempla* are so trite that they do not need to be assigned to specific sources, as when Lactantius mentions Menoeceus, Codrus, Curtius, and the (Decii) Mures as examples of patriotic self-sacrifice. Menoeceus and Codrus are mentioned in this way in Cicero (*Tusc. Disp.* 1.116), Codrus, Curtius, and the Decii in Valerius Maximus 5.6 and numerous other authors. Again, Mucius (Scaevola) and Regulus, linked as examples of heroism, were too common to need authorities. They recur time and time again in classical and patristic writing (Seneca, *Ep.* 24.3–11, 67.7–13, 98.12; Tertullian, *Mart.* 4; Min. Fel. 37). But there were also special collections of *exempla* made for the help of writers. The instances were grouped under headings (courage, piety, etc.) and embraced Greek and foreign as well as Roman cases. Cornelius Nepos had composed such a collection and others are known,[7] but the most famous was the still-surviving work of Valerius Maximus, dedicated to Tiberius soon after A.D. 31. It was widely used by the elder Pliny and scholars down to the end of antiquity. In fact two epitomes were made of it (by Paris and Nepotianus). Perhaps not unnaturally Lactantius does not cite him by name but there are good grounds for supposing that he used him or, at least, an edited version of a section of his work.

---

[6] M. Carlsson, *Class. Phil.* 43 (1948), 92–104.
[7] e.g. Augustus, Pomponius Rufus, Hyginus, Verrius Flaccus.

Brandt lists a number of possible borrowings but some of these can be dismissed.[8] The placation of Ceres during the Gracchan troubles (2.4.29 = V.M. 1.1.1) was also told by Cicero (*Verr.* 4.108) who is clearly the main source of this section of Lactantius, just as the accounts of Dionysius of Syracuse (2.4.27 = V.M. 1.1 ext.3) will come from Cicero, *de Nat. Deorum* 3.83 and of Archytas of Tarentum (*De Ira* 18.4) from Cicero, *Tusc. Disp.* 4.78. I also doubt whether Lactantius owed the story of the loyalty of the Pythagoreans (Damon and Pythias; 4.17.22–23) to Valerius (4.7 ext.1), because he does not name them and it was a very popular τόπος (Cicero, *Tusc. Disp.* 5.63; Diodorus Siculus 6.243; Iamblichus, *Pyth.* 33.234).

But other cases, which are less familiar, seem from very exact linguistic resemblance to be derived from a source close to Valerius. Furius Bibaculus' carrying of the *ancile* during his praetorship is quoted 'inter praecipua pietatis exempla' (1.21.47), 'cum haberet magistratus beneficio muneris eius vacationem', a phrase which mirrors Valerius' 'quamvis vacationem huius officii honoris beneficio haberet' (1.1.9). In the same way, a few pages later (1.22.5–6) he tells of the discovery by Q. Petilius of the two chests containing the body of Numa and some Greek and Latin writings. The story goes back ultimately to Livy (40.29) but Lactantius' account echoes Valerius' language (1.1.12) and omits many of the Livian details. The disastrous wrath of Juno against Terentius Varro before the battle of Cannae 'quod formosum puerum in tensa Iovis ad exuvias tenendas conlocaverat' (2.16.16) does not figure in Livy but is told, almost word for word, by Valerius (1.1.16).

The most striking list of *exempla*, however, comes at 2.7.7 (recapitulated in 2.16.11). It comprises three categories, the pious, the sacrilegious, and those visited by dreams. The examples of piety are Attus Navius, the appearance of Castor and Pollux, Vatienus, the story of Fortuna Muliebris, the story of Juno Moneta, Claudia, and the arrival of Aesculapius at Rome. Now there is a large lacuna in our manuscript text of Valerius from 1.1 ext. 4 to 1.5.2, but the greater part of the content can be recovered from the epitome, so that we know that Valerius

---

[8] See also Helm, *R.E.*, 'Valerius (239)', col. 114; Klotz, *Sitz. Bay. Akad. Wiss.* 5 (1942), 29–32.

dealt with Attus Navius in 1.4.1. But there are some peculiarities. In Valerius Maximus Castor and Pollux make two appearances, once 'bello Latino' at the Battle of Regillus and secondly,
much later, 'bello Macedonico apud lacum Iuturnae' (1.8.1):
Lactantius has conflated them (2.7.9) into one appearance
'bello Latino apud lacum Iuturnae'. Yet there are striking
similarities of language (e.g. 'sudorem abluentes'). Significantly
the story of Vatienus occurs in Valerius between these two
appearances (1.8.1). Fortuna Muliebris is dealt with in the
same chapter of Valerius (1.8.4: Lactantius omits *sed bis* but
that is not of importance). Iuno Moneta, invited to come to
Rome from Veii by Camillus, is, however, remarkable in that
only Lactantius and Valerius give her that epithet: it is not in
the original account in Livy (5.22). The version about Aesculapius is in substance the same in both authors (2.7.13 = 1.8.2)
but Valerius' is much fuller. The surprise is Claudia. The
miracle of her pulling the ship bearing the Idaean Mother with
her girdle was extremely famous[9] and was linked with the
appearance of Castor and Pollux and with the dream of
Latinus (see below) in other apologists (Tertullian, *Apol.* 22.12;
Min. Fel. 27.4), but it is not to be found in our text of Valerius.
Valerius did however know of Claudia. At 1.8.11 his text is
again fragmentary. He is talking of the miraculous survival of
statues after fires: 'quod deusto sacrario Saliorum nihil in eo
praeter lituum Romuli integrum repertum est; quod Servi
Tulli statua . . . in vestibulo templi Matris deum, bis ea aede
incendio consumpta in sua basi flammis intacta stetit'. Paris'
summary ('deusto sacrario Saliorum nihil in eo praeter lituum
repertum est incolume. Servii Tullii statua, cum aedes Fortunae
conflagrasset, inviolata mansit. Quintae Claudiae statua in
vestibulo templi deum Matris posita, bis ea aede incendio
consumpta, in flammis stetit') shows that the full text of Valerius
referred to Claudia and her story may have been told at that
point. Elsewhere, however, Valerius says that the stone of the
Idaean mother was summoned *Pythii Apollinis monitu* (8.15.3)
whereas Lactantius writes *ex libris Sibyllinis*. Nevertheless, on
balance it is hard to believe that Valerius did not somewhere
mention Claudia and her girdle.

[9] Cic. *Cael.* 34; Livy 29.14.12; Ovid, *Fasti* 4.305–44; Propertius 4.11.51 ff; Silius
17.23–45; Statius, *Silv.* 1.2.145 ff.

The sacrilegious pose few problems. Four, Ap. Claudius, Fulvius, Turullius, and Pyrrhus, were all recounted by Valerius Maximus (1.1.17, 1.1.19 (very similar), 1.1.20, and 1.1 ext. 1). The fifth, Alexander's soldiers at Miletus, comes in the missing section but there is a summary in Paris (1.1 ext. 5).

There are two dreams, Augustus and his doctor (1.7.1) and Latinius (1.7.4). The latter raises considerable complications. Before the games an unnamed man whipped his slave across the circus. The original story is found in Livy (2.36). A plebeian, named T. Latinius (so MP$^{cm}$: Latinus $\varDelta$), dreamt that Juppiter told him that the games must be held again, or disaster would occur. Latinius disregarded the dream and his son died. The dream recurred. Again he disregarded it and was attacked by disease. The third time he saw the dream, he told it to the consuls and was miraculously cured. In Valerius Maximus (1.7.4), the plebeian is called T. Latinius (P: Latinus B) and the other man remains unnamed, but in Lactantius he appears twice as Ti. Atinius and the slave-owner is called Autronius Maximus. The story also occurs in Macrobius (*Sat.* 1.11.3, not from Lactantius) where the man has become *Annius quidam* and the slave-owner is once again Autronius Maximus. There can hardly be any question of Valerius' text being defective. Yet the general similarities between this long section of Lactantius and Valerius are so strong that one can only conjecture that Lactantius knew a revised edition. In that connection it may well be no coincidence that all the allusions come from Book 1 of Valerius, a phenomenon which we have also seen in the case of Livy.

Finally, a word should be said about his knowledge of more antiquarian writers. Two passages (*D.I.* 7.14.8 on *septenarius numerus* and *De Op.* 8.10 on the sight of the mind) have parallels in Aulus Gellius, the author of the *Noctes Atticae* who died in A.D. 175, but both came ultimately from Varro, and Gellius is not cited as the authority. Lactantius may have used Varro at first hand but the contexts could equally support the belief that he found his material in the first case in a theosophistical work (see p. 54), and in the second in a commentary used also by Chalcidius on the *Timaeus*. Gellius is, however, named in the *Epitome* (24.5 *in libris Noctium Atticarum*). The reference is interesting on two counts. Firstly, the quotation is very long

(=A.G.7.1) and does not correspond to any section in the *Institutions* (it should come near 2.8.6). It deals with Chrysippus' argument that a good Providence could not create bad men. The inference must be that Lactantius came across the *Noctes Atticae* after the first edition of the *Institutions* had been published. This is confirmed by the fact that in the second edition of the *Institutions* (represented by the manuscripts RS) there is a long addition after 2.8.6 on the same topic, dealing with the spirit of Good and Evil. It does not mention Chrysippus or Aulus Gellius but does contain an unacknowledged quotation from A.G. 7.1—'alterum si tollas, utrumque sustuleris'. The first edition belongs between A.D. 305 and 311, the second to *c.* 324 (*D.I.* 1.1.13 ff.). Given Lactantius' movements and growing opportunities for consulting libraries between the two editions, such a conclusion is not surprising. Secondly, however, the copy of Aulus Gellius which Lactantius used differs substantially from that found in our surviving manuscript.[10] The variations point towards a careless and normalized text (cf. e.g. *insulsius* and *necesse*) but it is one that has no relationship to the Gellian stemma. It is, therefore, all the more unfortunate that the seventh-century palimpsest (A = Pal. Vat. XXIV) only covers Books 1–4, since it also has a radically different text from the transmitted one.

Verrius Flaccus is quoted once (*D.I.* 1.20.5 on Faula, the mistress of Hercules), but Verrius' learning on early Rome

---

[10] The major differences, according to the edition of C. Hosius (Leipzig, 1903), are as follows:

1. quibus non videtur . . . quam propter   *om.* Gellius
2. adversus ea   G : ad ea   Lact.
   insubidius   G : insulsius   L
   itidem   G : ibidem   L
3. necessum   G : necesse   L
   adverso quaeque   G : adversoque   L
4. posset   G : potest   L
   intemperantiae   G : intemperantia   L
   foret   G : forte   L
   contra   G : contraria   L
5. infortunitas   G : importunitas   L
   dolor et voluptas   G : voluptas et dolor   L
6. sicuti   G : sicut   L
   deligatum est   G : deligatum   L

The apparatus of the Oxford Classical Text edition (ed. P. K. Marshall, 1958) is less full. See Holford-Strevens, *Reallexicon f. Ant. n. Christ.*, 1052–3.

found its way into many commentaries (e.g. Servius, *ad Aen.* 8.203) and textbooks (e.g. Macrobius, *Sat.* 1.4, 1.6, 1.8, 1.10, etc.) and the subject was continually reworked. It is perhaps noteworthy that the only other authority (*D.I.* 1.20.36) for the worship of Caca, who betrayed her brother's theft, is in Servius (*ad Aen.* 8.190). Both go back to some common source. But if Verrius is unlikely to have been read at first hand, it is still less likely that Sinnius Capito was, who is also quoted once for his *Libri Spectaculorum* on the history of the names of the Games (6.20.35).[11] This work is also quoted several times by Festus (e.g. 186 L.) but its date is unknown. Sinnius also wrote letters on grammatical subjects (Aul. Gell. 5.21.9), the first of which was written to Pacuvius Labeo who died at the battle of Philippi in 48 B.C. There is nothing to exclude the possibility that Sinnius wrote his work on Games in the late Republic and that it was known to, and used by, Varro. Varro himself requires a separate discussion.

There is one rather exotic reference. At *D.I.* 1.22.19 he gives a substantial quotation in Latin from Didymus' *Libri ἐξηγήσεως Πινδαρικῆς* on the subject of Melissus and his daughters, Amalthea and Melissa.[12] Now with one exception (fr. 59 from Ammonius, *De Differentiis*) all the known fragments of Didymus' Commentary on Pindar come from the Scholiasts on Pindar's surviving poems. Indeed a closely related fragment (13), which accepted Timaeus' opinion that Mt. Atabyrios was in Sicily rather than in Rhodes, come from *Σ oe.* 7.87. It is related because in *D.I.* 1.22.23 he refers to Juppiter Ataburius and Juppiter Labryandius, which suggests that he found the names in the same note of Didymus. Now it can hardly be believed that Lactantius was the only writer in late antiquity who took the trouble to consult Didymus' work in the original. The allusion must be connected with the earlier allusion to Amalthea (1.21.38), which I argued (p. 13) came from a Commentary on the *Aratea*, incorporating quotations of Musaeus, Ovid, Cicero, and Germanicus. It is precisely in that way that Didymus' learning was disseminated and handed down, and it is in keeping that our surviving scholia on the

---

[11] R. Reitzenstein, *Verr. Forsch.* (Bresl. Phil. Abhand. 1.4 (1887)), 22, 80.

[12] M. Schmidt, *Didymi Chalcenteri Grammatici Fragmenta* (Leipzig, 1854), 220, fr. 14; see R. Pfeiffer, *History of Classical Scholarship* (Oxford, 1968), 276–7.

*Aratea* include references to such recondite authors as Aglaosthenes, Antisthenes, Artemidorus, Callimachus, Heraclides Ponticus, Myrtiles, Oenomaos, Pherecydes, Philiscus, Panyassis, and Zenodotus the Aetolian.

Two other writers should be mentioned. In 5.11.19 Lactantius quotes from the seventh book of Ulpian's *De Officio Proconsulis* on the subject of the rescripts of the emperors concerning penalties to be inflicted on Christians. Ulpian, the great jurist who died in A.D. 228, wrote ten books on the duties of a proconsul. The treatment of the Christians presumably came in the section on *sacrilegi*, from which another fragment survives grading the appropriate penalties (Lenel, *Palingenesia* ii, p. 275, fr. 2190). The legal situation was something which any Christian would have been bound to have known, especially one who felt the persecutions as deeply as Lactantius. Knowledge of the relevant section of a legal work does not imply familiarity with the work as a whole.

It would, equally, have been an essential ingredient of Lactantius' upbringing to have studied Quintilian, the great teacher of rhetoric, and the rhetorical exercises which passed under his name. Lactantius' familiarity with Quintilian's *Institutes* is seen in his quotation of a passage from Book 8, containing a Latin iambic trimeter (8.5.5 ∼ *D.I.* 3.17.32) and his allusions to the judgements on Cicero (10.1.123 ∼ *D.I.* 1.15.16) and Seneca (10.1. 128 ff. ∼ *D.I.* 5.9.19; cf. also 5.1.25). Only 145 out of at least 388 minor Declamations survive. It should not therefore cause concern if the two which Lactantius actually quotes and attributes to Quintilian—the *De Capite Obvoluto* (5.7.7) and the *Fanaticus* (1.21.17)—together with a third unplaced fragment (6.23.30)—are not in the extant corpus. Some fragments of a Latin declamation have been found in a third-century papyrus from Egypt.[13] But Lactantius does not use Quintilian extensively, because, for him, the rhetorical education which Quintilian represented was a failure, since it did not concern itself with *moral* excellence.

[13] R. Cavenaille, *Corpus Papyrorum Latinarum* (Wiesbaden, 1957), no. 65.

# V.  Varro and Euhemerus

BRANDT was almost alone in claiming that Lactantius did not
have direct knowledge of Varro.[1] Most other scholars have
accepted that the numerous references are genuine, for later
scholars certainly did have access to copies of many of his
writings. Some books of the *De Lingua Latina* and the *De Re
Rustica* still survive, and St. Augustine, Censorinus, and Macrobius, as well as grammarians, quote him at first hand. Yet the
evidence is awkward. Brandt gives twenty-seven citations.
Nine of these come from the first half of the *De Opificio* and
raise special questions which are not relevant here. Three of the
others are passing allusions on commonplace matters which do
not actually mention Varro and do not require any special
attachment (1.17.13 Erichthonius ἀπὸ τῆς ἔριδος καὶ χθόνος;
2.9.21 marriages with fire and water; 7.14.8 *septenarius numerus*:
see p. 25). In two further cases one can establish that Lactantius *cannot* actually have read Varro. The first is the oracle
of 'Apollo' at Dodona (p. 25). The second is the reference to
Lucretius and Varro on the four elements (2.12.4). As I have
argued elsewhere,[2] this must be Varro of Atax, but the plain
'Varro' in Lactantius can only be intended to refer to Varro
of Reate, so that he has not checked his references. In one
other unattributed quotation (3.17.29 the lion squashing the
mouse) the *poeta inanissimus* is Lucretius praising Epicurus:
Brandt's reference to Varro's *Eumenides* seems misplaced. Nor
can the citation of Tarquitius (1.10.2) be called as evidence.
It may come ultimately from Varro but Lactantius does not
mention Varro and it comes in a typical list of apologetic
attacks on the shortcomings of the gods.

The other quotations fall into two distinct categories: (1) the
long section on the Sibyls (1.6.7–12; cf. 4.15.27, *De Ira* 22.5)
which is expressly said to come from M. Varro's *Libri Rerum*

---

[1] *Wien. Stud.* 13 (1891), 255 ff. It can be shown that other Christian writers
knew Varro at second hand, e.g. Tertullian in the *De Spectaculis* (Waszink, *Vig.
Chris.* 2 (1948), 224 ff.). But see M. Perrin, op. cit., pp. 41 ff.

[2] *J.T.S.* 26 (1975), 411 ff.

*Divinarum quos ad C. Caesarem pontificem maximum scripsit*; (2) four
fragments on antiquarian matters where the author is simply
called Varro and the work from which the quotation comes is
not named.

The clearest example in the second category is 1.22.10 on
Faunus, where Varro is quoted between Gavius Bassus and
Sextus Clodius (see p. 39). The fact that Arnobius also deals
with the myths of Faunus and quotes Sextus Clodius suggests
that both he and Lactantius are drawing on a commonplace of
apologetic writing. One stage in the accumulation of these
different versions about Faunus may have been Cornelius
Labeo who is used as an authority on the subject by Macrobius
1.12.21. Interestingly, Macrobius cites the same passage of
Varro (1.12.27) but with greater specific detail and as a direct
quotation, whereas Lactantius only gives a paraphrase in
indirect speech. This confirms the impression that Lactantius
is not retailing Varro at first hand.

Another revealing example is 2.12.21–4 where Varro is
quoted on the question why the ancients were thought to have
lived for 1,000 years and argues that the Egyptians regarded
months as years. This was a topic that appealed to Varro who
discusses expectation of life in several places. In the *libri fatales*,
for instance, he propounded the view that the norm of human
life was 84 (12 × 7) and elsewhere quoted the evidence of
Alexandrian embalmers for the fact that men could not live for
more than 100 years.[3] Censorinus (*De Die Natali* 17) is our
main first-hand authority for Varro's theories on the subject,
but there are some significant clues in Lactantius himself which
indicate once again that he has not gone directly to Varro for
his testimony. In the first place the passage is only a reported
quotation (*ait enim* + Or. Obl.); secondly, as in the previous
example, Varro is quoted as one among other authorities who
give a different view, namely that men usually live 120 years.
But the chief pointers are given by the context of the passage
and by the slight variation in the *Epitome* (22.5). Lactantius
states that he is raising a matter now which he will deal with
fully at the end of the work—that is the whole question of

---

[3] The same data in Pliny, *N.H.* 7.48; Augustine, *C.D.* 15.12; Diomedes 1.375 K.
The passage came from the *Antiquitates Rerum Humanarum*; see F. Franceschi,
*Aevum* 28 (1954), 408.

millenarianism. Before the Fall Man's life-span was indefinite or at least 1,000 years. It was Adam's Fall that abbreviated his life to a mere 930 years (Genesis 5:5) and after the Flood 120 years became the limit. The whole of the discussion, therefore, is firmly set against a background of millenarianism, which first gained popularity at the beginning of the Christian era as the result of the cross-fertilization of Hellenic and Iranian speculations, and which was proclaimed first by 'Hystaspes' (see p. 54) before passing into a lively, if heterodox, tradition of the church, almost whose last exponent was Lactantius himself. We are therefore dealing again with a ready-made argument.

1.13.8 is less clear cut. It is at once obvious that Lactantius has simply taken over the mention of Diodorus, Thallus, Nepos, and Cassius from Minucius Felix (21.4; see p. 38), but he adds Varro and it is a reasonable inference that it was Varro who did the necessary research into the two Greek and two Latin authors in the first place, and it could be argued that Lactantius is showing off his scholarship by repeating Minucius and adding Varro to demonstrate that he knew where Minucius had got all his facts from, and that he himself had also studied the great Roman antiquary. But I doubt it. If you compare the very elaborate details quoted from Varro by Macrobius (*Sat.* 1.7 and 8) with this bald statement, I think that the very utmost that can be inferred is that Varro was well known to be the principal Roman authority. Here again it is not only Arnobius (*Adv. Nat.* 3.29) who reminds us that we are dealing with very hackneyed material.[4]

If after this one were to believe that Lactantius combed the pages of Varro to discover that Samos was once called Parthenia (1.17.8)—a commonplace frequently repeated from the time of Callimachus (*H.* 4.49 cf. fr. 599 Pf.) and Aristotle (fr. 570 R.) onwards, Lactantius would indeed have succeeded in deceiving his readers. It is a schoolmaster's knowledge, just as Servius quotes Varro for an eccentric etymology of Libya (*ad Aen.* 1.22).

The long catalogue of the Sibyls (1.6.7–12) is another matter. It is quoted with a precise indication of the source. The same

---

[4] Minucius had leant on Tertullian, *Apol.* 10.7 who betrays *his* second hand sources by giving Cassius the *cognomen* Severus rather than Hemina. He also adds to the two Greek and two Roman authors an open-ended mention of 'ullus commentator eiusmodi antiquitatum'. Varro would spring to mind.

evidence, slightly corrupted, occurs in the anonymous preface to our collection of the Sibylline Oracles, but it is virtually certain that this is very late and simply amplified from Lactantius himself (see Geffcken ad loc.)[5] There are, however, other traces of this famous passage.

The most relevant, because the closest to Varro in time, is Tibullus 2.5.67 ff.:

> Quicquid Amalthea, quicquid Marpesia dixit
>   Herophile, Phoeto Graia quod admonuit,
> Quasque Aniena sacras Tiburs per flumina sortes
>   Portavit sicco.

> Phyto *Huscke*: phoebo *codd.* Graia *Lachmann*: grata *codd.*

B. Cardauns[6] has argued convincingly not only for the text as printed but also for its immediate derivation from Varro. Tibullus quotes only four Sibyls but that was all that the context of his poem to Messalinus required.

1. Amalthea = *D.I.* 1.6.10. The seventh Sibyl.
2. Marpesia Herophile. *D.I.* 1.6.10 gives Herophile or Demophile as alternative names of Amalthea and 1.6.12 names the eighth Sibyl as 'Hellespontia in agro Troiano nata, vico Marmesso'. As Maass saw,[7] Marmesso is a corruption of Marpesso, but not a scribal corruption.
3. Phoeto. The name is also recorded as a Sibyl name by Clement of Alexandria (*Strom.* 1.21) and by the author of the Tübingen *Theosophy* (see below) as the name of the sixth Sibyl—the Samian Sibyl left anonymous by Lactantius (1.6.9).
4. Aniena Tiburs = *D.I.* 1.6.12.[8] The tenth Sibyl is 'Tiburtem nomine Albuneam, quae Tiburi colatur iuxta ripas amnis Anienis.'

If Tibullus is using Varro, then his text of Varro differs from Lactantius in naming Phoeto and Herophile and in the correct Marpesia. But there is a second witness—the Tübingen *Theosophy* (§73). Here there is an abbreviated account, with close similarities to the Sibylline Prologue but without any reference to Lactantius. Indeed there are significant differences

---

[5] Lactantius seems also to have been the source of Jerome, *Ad Iovin.* 1.2.306 D; Augustine, *C.D.* 18.23.

[6] *Hermes* 89 (1961), 357 ff.

[7] *De Sibyllarum Indicibus*, 33.

[8] See, most recently, R.E.A. Palmer, *Roman Religion and Roman Empire*, 80–9.

here too from the Varronian account, as reported by Lactantius: 'Sibyl' is said to be a word of Ῥωμαϊκὴ λέξις; the price of the Sibylline Books is given as 100, not 300 Philippics; Phoeto is again mentioned by name.[9]

The convergence of evidence suggests that neither Lactantius nor the *Theosophy* is quoting Varro direct or in full, although both ultimately go back to him. Further light may be thrown on this by considering the last of the prophetic authorities used by Lactantius—Hystaspes or Hydaspes, one of the spurious Magi whose works were fashionable under the empire.[10] Hystaspes was known to Justin (*Apol.* 20.1, 44.12), Clement of Alexandria (*Strom.* 6.5), and Johannes Lydus (*De Mens.* 2.14). He is extensively quoted by Lactantius in the eschatology of Book 7 (14–17). In outline, his 'oracle' was a dream of a prophetic boy,[11] who foresaw that the world would last for 6,000 years and end in calamities of all sorts, including the fall of the Roman empire. This stage would be succeeded by a millennium of peace, when even the animals would be at one with each other.

Two points are immediately clear. The original oracle must have been in Greek for it to be cited by Justin and Clement. Nevertheless, secondly, it is obviously influenced by Varronian speculation on the *septenarius numerus*, which led him for instance to invent the canon of the seven hills of Rome.[12] Lydus indeed quotes part of the oracle which equated the number of planets with the number of days in the week—a key step in Varro's theory (*De Mens.* 2.14). What language did Lactantius know it in? The only two actual quotations are both in indirect speech: 'pios ac fideles a nocentibus segregatos . . . impios extincturum' (7.18.2) and 'sublatum iri ex orbe imperium nomenque Romanum' (7.15.19). We have no other evidence for a Latin translation of Hystaspes and since elsewhere Lactantius quotes the Sibylline Oracles in indirect speech in what is clearly his own translation (e.g. 7.15.18 = *O.S.* 8.171–3), the only reasonable hypothesis is that Lactantius knew Hy-

---

[9] Erbse, *Fragmente griech. Theosophien*, 40–1.

[10] H. Windisch, *Verhand. Akad. Wetensch.* 28 (1929); Bidez-Cumont, *Les Mages hellénisés* 1. 215–7; Momigliano, *Alien Wisdom*, 146; V. Fabrege, *Bonn. Jährb. f. Antike und Christentum* 17 (1974).

[11] A very oriental feature; cf. Daniel 2:31.

[12] R. Gelsomino, *Varrone e i sette colle di Roma* (1974).

staspes also in Greek. The Tübingen *Theosophy* combines Sibylline Oracles, Oracles of the Clarian Apollo (p. 22) and Hystaspes, as well as Varronian data on the Sibyls and extraneous material. Now some of this at least is ultimately due to Porphyry's compilation, but, as has been shown above (p. 24), there must have been an intermediary between Porphyry and the *Theosophy*, a Christian intermediary, and that same intermediary will have been used by Lactantius, who was not himself acquainted with Porphyry. It is, therefore, a reasonable conjecture that this Christian compiler had already grouped together Hystaspes with the Sibylline and Clarian oracles, and the Varronian catalogue of Sibyls. But the compilation must have been in Greek. Now, although Lactantius' quotation does indeed specify the title of the precise work of Varro's, it does not give an exact quotation. It is in indirect speech and there are no distinctively Varronian turns of phrase. I conclude, therefore, that this long catalogue has its immediate source in the same Greek 'theosophistic' compilation. Even if Lactantius did derive it directly from Varro, there is nothing to suggest that he had read anything else of the *Libri Rerum Divinarum*.

One of the richest treasures of Lactantius is his liberal use of the *Sacred History* of Euhemerus of Messene.[13] Euhemerus, writing towards the end of the fourth century, B.C., was the author of a rationalistic history of the gods, which aimed to show how the gods were only great men honoured for their deeds (Cicero, *N.D.* 1.119; Plutarch, *De Iside* 360 a; Min.Fel. 21.1 *et al.*). The book enjoyed a certain *succès de scandale* and was translated into Latin by no less a person than Ennius himself (Cicero, loc. cit.). Almost all our knowledge of Ennius' version comes from the *D.I.*, apart from one quotation in Varro (F 26 'gluma: id apud Ennium solum scriptum scio esse in Euhemeri libris versis'), one in Augustine (F 17 '(in Olympo) Iovem castra posuisse cum adversus patrem bella gereret, ut ea docet historia quam vestri etiam Sacram vocant'), and three doubtful allusions in Columella and Pliny (F 27–9). The scope of the original was obviously wide. It dealt primarily with Juppiter (there are two substantial fragments in Diodorus

---

[13] The fullest account is by Jacoby, *R.E.*, s.v. Testimonia and fragments in Jacoby, *Fr. G. Hist.* 63. See also G. Vallauri, Pubbl. Fac. Lett. e Fil. Torino 1960; K. Thaede, *R.L.A.C.* 6 (1965), 877–90; S. Spyridakis, *C.J.* 63 (1968), 337; M. Brozek, *Meander* 24 (1969), 455–97; 25 (1970), 249–61.

(F 2–3), one of which contains a long account of Juppiter Triphylius at Panchaea in Arabia; cf. *D.I.* 1.11.33) but Minucius implies that other gods, such as Apollo, Isis, and Ceres were also discussed. It is not absolutely certain that Ennius translated the whole of the *Sacred History*, since, with the exception of F 25, the remaining fragments of his translation are only concerned with Juppiter himself.

Euhemerus was quickly adopted by the Christians as a weapon to beat the pagans at their own game. The first Apologist to invoke him was perhaps Clement of Alexandria (*Protrept.* 2.24), followed by Minucius, Theophilus (*Ad Autol.* 3.7), and Arnobius (*Adv. Nat.* 4.29). He was still popular in the fourth century when Eusebius and Augustine make use of him. Eusebius naturally quotes the Greek original. Laughton and Fraenkel have settled once and for all the issue of whether Lactantius is giving the actual words of his source.[14] On stylistic grounds F 12, 14, 15, 16, 19, 20, and 24 ( = I, III, IV, VI, VII, VIII, and XI Vahlen) clearly preserve archaic (or archaizing) language, while the other fragments, usually in indirect speech and not explicitly introduced as being the words of Ennius, are paraphrases. But whether the actual words are the words of Ennius is not resolved. It remains very strange that Ennius should have written a *prose* translation (it is against all the criteria of genres of his time) and, even apart from the fact that the fragments can be so easily rearranged as verse, the actual vocabulary belongs not to the style of prose-writers such as the elder Cato, but to the world of the stage.

It is, indeed, surprising that alone of Christian writers, Lactantius should show familiarity with the actual text of Ennius. The possibility must not be ruled out *a priori*, but it is worth looking at the contexts in which Euhemerus is cited. Of the thirteen passages, six occur in *D.I.* 1.11, two in *D.I.* 1.13, three in *D.I.* 1.14, and one each in *D.I.* 1.17 and 1.22. The last passage (F 10) follows immediately on the quotation from Didymus about Amalthea and Melissa (see p. 48) and deals with Juppiter Ataburius and Juppiter Labryandius, which were also treated by Didymus. Three of the passages in *D.I.* 1.11 (63 and

---

[14] *Eranos* 49 (1951), 35–56. The methodology for distinguishing genuine quotations from paraphrases is further developed by M. Lausberg, *Untersuchungen zu Senecas Fragmenta*, esp. p. 188 on the resumptive *igitur/ergo*.

$65 = F$ 13, 18, 21) bracket the note of Aglaosthenes which is said to come from 'Caesar in Arato' (see p. 13)—in fact, a commentary on the *Aratea*. Indeed the whole of *D.I.* 1.11, as Maass pointed out,[15] bears the mark of a Stoic commentary on the mythology of Juppiter. It has a very great deal in common with Aristides' *Hymn of Jupiter*, Cornutus' *De Iove* and, above all, the $\Sigma$ on Germanicus, *Aratea*. Given the fact that Lactantius' use of Ennius–Euhemerus is circumscribed to these few chapters and this particular context, I am very strongly inclined to believe that an *Aratea* commentary was the immediate source of almost all the material. If so, it must have been an extensive and well-documented commentary but it is once again relevant to note that Hyginus, who condensed such a commentary or commentaries, three times gives Euhemerus as an authoritative source (*Poet. Astr.* 2.12, 13, 42 = F 4, 5, 7). Once the possibility of an intermediary is admitted, then we must accept that Lactantius is no longer evidence for the belief that Ennius translated Euhemerus into prose.[16]

[15] *Aratea*, 252.
[16] In his recent edition of Varro's *Antiquitates Rerum Divinarum* (Wiesbaden, 1976), B. Cardauns discusses the list of Sibyls ( = fr. 56 a/b) and argues for direct derivation from Varro but without evidence. See also A. Mancini, *Studi Storici* 5 (1896), 229 ff.; H. Jagielski, *De Lactantii fontibus* (Diss. Königsberg, 1912).

# VI.   Cicero

Of all classical authors Cicero had the greatest and deepest influence on Lactantius both as a stylist and as a thinker.[1] No survey of his reading could be complete without some analysis of the debt that Lactantius owed to his philosophical and other writings, for, even before Pico della Mirandola claimed that Lactantius equalled and perhaps surpassed Cicero in eloquence,[2] Jerome had called attention to that 'stream of Ciceronian eloquence' (*Epist.* 58.10 'fluvio eloquentiae Tullianae'). The purpose of this chapter is to examine the range of his reading and, where possible, the textual traditions to which he had access.

## Lost or fragmentary works

As is well known, Cicero published two editions of the *Academica* in 45 B.C. The first edition consisted of the dialogues *Hortensius*, *Catulus*, and *Lucullus*. Of these the *Hortensius* enjoyed great popularity but is now lost together with the almost unknown *Catulus*, while the *Lucullus* ( = *Academica Priora*) survives. Later in the year he revised the work. The *Hortensius*, which may have been published separately and earlier, was left unaffected but Cicero rewrote the *Catulus* and *Lucullus*, making the main interlocutors at first perhaps Cato and Brutus, and then Varro and Atticus, as well as himself. The final version, dedicated to Varro, survives only as a fragment, comprising part of what was the original *Catulus* ( = *Academica Posteriora*).

Lactantius was certainly familiar with the *Hortensius* (see p. 60). His citations help us in fact to reconstruct the scope and contents of the dialogue.[3] But, surprisingly, it appears that

---

[1] A. Trevale, *Cicero e Lattanzio* (Diss. Catania, 1946); H. Blumenberg, *Studium Generale* 12 (1959), 485 ff. with bibliography; G. Gawlick, *Studia Patristica* 9 (1966), 57–62; T. Wojtczak, *De Lactantio Ciceronis aemulo* (Warsaw, 1969).

[2] *De Studio Divinae atque Humanae Philosophiae* 1.7.

[3] The best edition is by A. de Grilli (1962); for a recent study see C. Vitelli, *Hermes* 104 (1976), 59 ff., with bibliography, especially on connections with the *Pro Archia*. We should add *D.I.* 3.16.1–3 as a fragment of the *Hortensius* not the *De Republica* (Grilli p. 129). For a discussion of the background of 3.2.3–10 (against

he did not know the *Catulus* and *Lucullus* but only the latest
revision, the *Academica Posteriora*. Three quotations correspond
with our surviving portion of that work. Of these 3.14.13
( = *Ac. Post.* 1.3) and 3.29.7 ( = *Ac. Post.* 1.45) are very general
paraphrases which can throw no light on the state of the text,
but 3.29.3 (on Fortune) gives a verbatim citation: 'quod multa
inquit Cicero efficiat inopinata nobis propter obscuritatem
ignorationemque causarum' = *Ac. Post.* 1.29 'quod efficiat multa
improvisa ac necopinata nobis propter obscuritatem ignorationemque causarum'. The manuscripts of Cicero read *hec;*
Halm's *ac* is probably preferable to the reading *et* of the later
manuscripts and no significance should be attached to the
variation in the order of the words *multa efficiat*. What is of
interest is Lactantius' substitution of 'inopinata' for 'improvisa
ac necopinata', which is a typical instance of simplification and
also of the tendency to normalize language, since the form
*necopinatus* was not current in his day and, indeed, is not found
after Florus (see my note on Livy 3.26.5).

Two quotations correspond to passages of the surviving
*Lucullus*. 7.23.3 ('Chrysippus qui fulcire putatur porticum
Stoicorum') has a loose resemblance to *Lucullus* 75. 7.4.11 is
more revealing: respondendum est Ciceroni qui ait: 'cur deus
omnia nostra causa cum faceret, tantam vim natricum vipera-
rumque fecerit? cur tam multa pestifera terra marique disper-
serit?' The relevant passage of the *Lucullus* (120) agrees except
for reading 'cur mortifera tam multa ⟨ac *add.* Reid; et *add.*
Halm⟩ perniciosa terra . . .' Now it is possible that the variant is
due to carelessness by Lactantius (*pes/tifera; mortifera/perniciosa*)
but *pestifer* is a good Ciceronian word (e.g. *N.D.* 2.120) and it
seems, therefore, more likely that Lactantius is here also quoting
from the *Academica Posteriora* and not from the *Lucullus*. This
hypothesis is confirmed by *D.I.* 6.24.2: '[Ciceronis] in Aca-
demico tertio verba sunt: quodsi liceret ut eis qui in itinere
deerravissent, sic vitam deviam secutis corrigere errorem paeni-
tendo, facilior esset emendatio temeritatis.' The quotation looks
precise enough but the only parallel in the *Lucullus* is close in

philosophy) and possible Ciceronian influence see O. Gigon, *Romanitas et Christianitas* (Amsterdam, 1973), 145–79. J. S. Reid's edition of the *Academica* is still funda-
mental. See also the very acute discussion of *D.I.* 6.2.13–15 by P. Monat, *Rev.
ét. lat.* 53 (1975), 248 ff.

sense but not in language (9)—'sed nescioquo modo plerique errare malunt *et al.*'—and, as Reid argued, the Lactantius fragment is probably part of the revised introduction to Book 3 of the *Academica Posteriora*. One other fragment (*D.I.* 3.14.15 'mihi autem . . . hebetes et obtunsi'; note the allusion to *Academica* in the preceding sentence), has no point of reference, and the phrase 'hebetes et obtunsi' is not otherwise attested in Cicero,[4] but the contents would be appropriate for Cicero's speech in Book 2.

The *Hortensius*, therefore. But the *Academica Posteriora*, not the *Catulus* and *Lucullus*. In this he is at one with Augustine and the late grammarians, but the earlier edition did survive. Quintilian knew both versions (3.6.64) and Ammianus, remarkably, appears to know only the earlier. This was, perhaps, a hazard of the book-trade.

The *Consolatio*, also composed in 45 B.C., has close ties with the *Hortensius*,[5] but whereas the *Hortensius* was only in very general terms modelled on Aristotle's *Protrepticus*, the *Consolatio* belongs to a much more stereotyped genre, the most influential exponent of which was Crantor.[6] This is not to say that Cicero followed Crantor slavishly but rather that the themes were much more traditional and predictable (cf. Cicero, *Tusc. Disp.* 3.81). It seems certain that Lactantius knew it in its entirety. The work opened with a strange assertion that men are born to pay for their sins (3.18.18 'in principio . . . luendorum scelerum causa nasci homines') and that we are possessed by error and ignorance of the truth (3.14.20 'nescioqui nos teneat error ac miserabilis ignoratio veri'; repeated at 3.18.18 with the words *recte praefatus*).[7] The sins are presumably in this life, the payment hereafter, since another fragment (15 = 3.19.6) distinguishes the abodes of the just and the impious. But Lactantius says that Cicero made the same point later in the work (*iteravit postea*) and he quotes passages on human beings who

[4] Cf. Seneca, *Epist.* 95.36; Val. Max. 6.9.1; Arnobius, *Adv. Nat.* 2.22.

[5] Grilli, p. 118.

[6] The latest collection of fragments is by K. Kumaniecki, *A.C.D.* 4 (1968) 27–47. See also Van Wageningen, *De Ciceronis libro consolationis* (Groningen, 1916); R. Kassel, *Untersuchungen zur griechischen und römischen Konsolationsliteratur*, Zetemata Heft 18 (Munich, 1958); Philippson, *Berl. phil. Woch.* (1917), 496 ff; J. Doignon, *R.E.L.* 51 (1973), 208–19.

[7] Frs. 10 and 12 Müller: but, as Brink points out (*J.R.S.* 51 (1961), 220), Müller has placed these fragments far too late.

have been received into the company of the gods (fr. 14 = *D.I.* 1.15.16–20) and on resistance to the blows of fortune (fr. 16 = *D.I.* 3.28.6). None of his quotations, however, overlaps with those of other authors so that we can say nothing about the state of the text which he had. How long the *Consolatio* survived is uncertain. Jerome (*Epist.* 60) and Ambrose (*De Excessu Fratris*) appear to refer to it but Doignon has argued that they were not quoting directly but only at second hand from Lactantius, whose adverse comments on the work may have hastened its disappearance. Boethius certainly did not know it. For our purpose, however, it is enough to shew that Lactantius was familiar with it.

The *De Legibus*—another work from the same period—raises different issues.[8] The truncated text that we have is preserved in two groups of manuscripts—H (Leidensis Heinsianus H 118; 11th c.) and A (Leidensis Vossianus A 84: 9th c.), B (Leidensis Vossianus B 86; 10th c.). It ends at Book 3.12, but the complete work probably contained 6 books on the analogy of the *De Republica*. Macrobius quotes from Book 5 so that there was at least one more or less complete text circulating in late antiquity. Apart from 2.1.14–19 on *status rectus*, not explicitly attributed and a commonplace in Lactantius, there are a few secondary paraphrases (e.g. *D.I.* 2.10.1 = 1.25, but note that Lactantius 'omnibus' disproves de Plinval's supplement ⟨plerasque⟩; 6.11.16 = 1.48). Some of the explicit quotations show no significant variation from the transmitted text of Cicero (*D.I.* 2.11.16 = 1.22; 6.25.9 = 1.28; 6.11.14 = 1.48 (*benignius-que/ve*); 5.20.3 = 2.19 (deliberate alteration of position of *caste*); 6.25.1 = 2.45). Others have to be considered separately.

a. 3.10.7 (7.9.10) = 1.24–25 ex tot generibus nullum est animal praeter hominem quod habeat notitiam aliquam dei, ipsisque in hominibus nulla gens est neque tam mansueta neque tam fera quae non etiamsi ignoret qualem habere deum deceat, tamen habendum sciat. ex quo efficitur ut is agnoscat deum qui unde ortus sit quasi recordetur.

habere *Lact.*: haberi *Cic. recte.*
ut *Lact.*: illud ut *Cic. recte*

---

[8] The latest accessible text is that of de Plinval in the Budé series but it has serious shortcomings. See the review by Nisbet, *C.R.* 10 (1960), 228; P. L. Schmidt's *Die Überlieferung von Ciceros Schrift 'De Legibus'* (Munich, 1974) has been adversely criticized.

recordetur *Lact.*: recordetur agnoscat *A*: recordetur cognoscat *BH*

The first two variants represent carelessness on Lactantius' part; the third may be the result of the incorporation of a dittography *ag/cognoscat* on the earlier *agnoscat* by the manuscript tradition of Cicero.

b. 1.15.23, 20.19, 5.20.3 = 2.19 divos et eos qui caelestes semper habiti sunt colunto et ollos quos endo caelo merita locaverunt . . . Quirinum. ast olla propter quae datur homini ascensus in caelum . . . delubra sunto.
    locaverunt *Lact.*: locaverint *G*: vocaverint *ABH*
    homini *Lact.*, *Cic.*: hominibus *de Plinval perperam*

*Loco* is clearly the right verb and the parallelism with *habiti sunt* shows that *locaverunt* must be the right tense.

c. 1.20.16 virtutes enim oportere non vitia consecrare = 2.28 virtutes enim non vitia consecrari decet.
    non vitia *H*: et vitia *AB*

Lactantius has adapted the text to or. obl. (*oportere*) but *consecrare* is a mistake. On the other hand his text is closer to H than to AB.

The passages show that Lactantius had a better text of the *De Legibus* than survives in our manuscripts. It is closest to H.

There are, however, also a number of other quotations which have no counterpart in our existing texts, but their contents enable us to place them with some certainty.

a. 5.8.10 [Cicero] disputans de legibus 'sicut una' inquit 'eademque natura . . . homines viverent'.

The argument from the natural kinship of the universe and destructive depravity of man must, as all scholars are agreed, have come early in the work, from one of the gaps in Book I.

b. 1.20.14 magnum Cicero audaxque consilium suscepisse Graeciam dicit, quod Cupidinum et Amorum simulacra in gymnasiis consecrasset.

Again the *De Legibus* is not named but, as Vahlen saw, the passage fits perfectly in the gap between chapters 23 and 24 of Book I and the jesting reference to Atticus, one of the interlocutors in the dialogue, makes the identification virtually certain.

c. 3.19.2 gratulemurque . . . profecto est mali.

Here the *De Legibus* is named and again Vahlen perceptively saw that the passage fitted in the lacuna between chapters 53 and 54 of Book 2.

Lactantius, therefore, does not cite any passage beyond Book 2 and it seems a fair inference that he had a text, not unlike H's, which lacked the last three or four books. If this is true, it is of crucial importance for the history of the transmission of the *De Legibus*.

The *De Republica* is a dialogue with close affinities to the *De Legibus* but it was composed nearly ten years earlier, in 54 B.C. Apart from the final book (Book 6 = the Somnium Scipionis) which has an independent tradition, only about a quarter of the work survives, preserved in a fourth-century palimpsest discovered by A. Mai in A.D. 1819. To this and to quotations in grammarians and patristic writers (Ambrose and Augustine as well as Lactantius) we owe our knowledge of its contents. Brandt lists 35 borrowings by Lactantius but his figure is over-optimistic and needs revision.[9] Several of the allusions do not specify the *De Republica* at all and could well be to other works: e.g. 1.9.1, 6.17.3, 6.19.4 (cf. *Tusc. Disp.* 3.25), 6.12.11, 3.16.1–3 (from the *Hortensius*: Grilli p. 119), 3.16.5 (from the *Hortensius*: Usener, *Gött. Gel. Anz.* 1892, 385), 3.19.13, 6.10.18–22 (from Lucretius 5.805 ff.), 5.14.15, 6.9.2–4. Others are not verbatim quotations but only very general references to the subject-matter (1.15.23, 7.10.10, 1.11.5 *docti indoctique*; 5.14.3–5, 5.16.2–4, 5.16.5–13).

Others, however, do give a literal text, sometimes coinciding with surviving portions of the palimpsest, sometimes not. The reliability of Lactantius' citations can therefore be checked partly by the palimpsest and partly by the corroboration of other authors who cite the same passage.

Only three passages directly overlap.

a. 6.9.6 = *De Rep.* 1.3 'ut . . . ut ait philosophus, sua sponte faciant quod legibus facere coguntur' = 'ut id sua sponte facerent quod cogerentur facere legibus.'

Lactantius has adjusted the syntax and word-order to fit his own context.

---

[9] D. Krarup, *Class. et Med.* 21 (1960), 20–8.

b. 1.15.31–32 = *De Rep.* 1.64, 2.20.

This passage, dealing with the apotheosis of Romulus and quoting Ennius, is a highly controversial one. I think it is likely that Lactantius has conflated two passages of the *De Rep.* together with memories of Livy 1.8 (note especially *habitu augustiorem*). This view rests on the fact that the final sentence ('eumque mandasse ad populum ut sibi delubrum fieret, se deum esse et Quirinum vocari') is a virtual transcription of *De Rep.* 2.20 ('eum sibi mandasse ut populum rogaret ut sibi eo in colle delubrum fieret; se deum esse et Quirinum vocari'). If this is correct, then the Ennius quotation, as I have argued (p. 9), came from Cicero and not directly from Ennius or some other source. The textual variations are to be explained by the fact that Lactantius is quoting from memory and not purporting to give a verbatim extract from the *De Rep.*

c. 5.12.5 = *De Rep.* 3.27. Lactantius, without naming the book, quotes a long passage from a speech of Furius against justice, on the subject of the misfortunes which a good man can encounter. The latter part of the quotation '[extermi]netur, egeat . . . esse malit' is preserved in the Ciceronian palimpsest and comes from Book 3. There are two significant variants: Lactantius omits *optima* (which is necessary for the clausula) and reads *denique* for *undique* (a careless metathesis). Given the length of the quotation, it is likely that he is quoting not from memory but from a text, a text that is inferior to the palimpsest.

There are four passages where the palimpsest is not extant.

a. 6.8.6–9 on Divine Law, which is said to come from Book 3 (33) and will have been spoken by Laelius. It contains at least one recognizable error. Of the manuscripts, B reads *interpresalius* (add. e B$^c$ $^{s.l.}$), R *interpres Laelius*. As Brandt saw, the true reading must be *Sextus Aelius*, the legal commentator.

To this passage should be added the later Ciceronian quotation in 6.24.29 which is not explicitly claimed for the *De Rep.* and has indeed been placed among the fragments of the *De Legibus*: 'illa lex dei praeclara et divina semper quae recta et honesta iubet, vetat prava et turpia'. The language is authentic (cf. *N.D.* 2.148; *De Domo* 148) and the argument follows closely on the earlier passage.

b. 5.18.4–8 contains some further scattered sentences from

Laelius' speech but there is no extensive quotation to show more
than the general argument. Cf. 5.22.7.

c. 5.11.2 'etenim si nemo est quin emori malit ... praestabilior
est animus corpore'. The argument about the relative value of
human and animal bodies and souls is attributed simply to
'M. Tullius'. The opening of Book 4, the 'aptior dicendi locus'
referred to in 2.48, would be a natural place for it (cf. *De Opif.*
1.11–13) but Wilsing[10] and others have placed it after 3.33
( = a. above).

d. 3.21.1–12, on Plato's Communism, contains several remarks of 'Socrates' which correspond to passages of Plato's
*Republic* but are more likely to have come from Cicero. For
Nonius (362.11 L. 'et noster Plato omnia qui prorsus iubet
esse communia ne quis civis propriam aut suam rem ullam
queat dicere'), by his independent quotation, shows that Cicero
dealt with the whole subject in Book 4. Again, however, Lactantius' extracts are too brief and too random to enable us to
form any inferences about the nature of the copy which he used.
But he certainly had a complete text.[11]

The two volumes *De Gloria*, written in 44 B.C. (*ad Att.* 16.16.1)
did not survive into the Middle Ages.[12] Indeed the last certain
excerpt from them was made by Aul. Gellius (15.6.1). Shackleton Bailey does indeed speak of 'citations in St. Jerome's letters'
in his commentary on the passage of *ad Att.* but I have not been
able to trace these. St. Jerome does, in his commentary on the
Galatians (5:26), allude to 'Ciceronis duo volumina quae de
gloria scripsit' but he shows no awareness of their contents, any
more than Lactantius does in his solitary reference to the work
(*D.I.* 1.15.16). I suspect that it did not survive beyond the
second century apart from lexicographical niceties handed
down to late grammarians.

One intriguing work has to be dismissed—Cicero's letters to
his son Marcus. These were known to Quintilian (1.7.34) and
Plutarch (*Cic.* 24), and grammatical peculiarities were preserved, but it is doubtful if even Plutarch had a text of them,
since the only allusion that he makes is to Cicero's commonplace advice συμφιλοσοφεῖν Κρατίππῳ. Between Plutarch and

[10] N. Wilsing, *Aufbau und Quellen von Ciceros Schrift de Republica* (Leipzig, 1929).
[11] See also the discussion on Cyprian as a possible source of Lactantius' views
on the theatre: p. 89.
[12] Manitius, *Ges. lat. Lit. Mittelalters* 1.479.

Lactantius there is silence about them, and indeed Lactantius' mention must be derivative ('philosophiae quidem praecepta noscenda, vivendum autem est civiliter'), since it is in indirect speech and uses the non-Ciceronian word *civiliter*, first in Aul. Gell. *Praef.* 13. The quotation became a mere popular saying (cf. Don. *ad Ter. Adelph.* 418).

## The Philosophical Works

The *De Natura Deorum* made the greatest impact.[13] The eighteen specific extracts in the *D.I.* are only a very small portion of the total debt. The subject-matter, treatment, and style of the dialogue naturally drew Lactantius to it and its influence pervades the whole of his thinking. Arnobius, Ambrose, Jerome, and Augustine[14] all knew it but none used it so extensively.

The surviving manuscripts, of which the primary ones seem to be A (Leidensis Vossianus 84: 9th c.), P (Vat. Pal. 1519: 10th c.), V (Vienna Hofbibliothek $\Phi$ 189/208: 9th c.), B (Leidensis Vossianus 86: 10th c.), and H (Leidensis Heinsianus 118: 11th c.), all derive from a common archetype which had a large lacuna at 3.65 where Cicero dealt with arguments subverting religion and a smaller lacuna at 3.13. The archetype (Q) must belong to the late fourth or fifth century since the missing passages were known to and quoted from by Arnobius, Servius, Diomedes, and the Verona $\Sigma$ on Virgil, as well as Lactantius. It has been claimed that the mutilation was deliberately done by Christians[15] but the evidence suggests rather that Christian scholars vented such disapproval not on classical authors but on erring and unorthodox co-religionists.[16] The omissions will have been caused by the ordinary accidents of transmission.

Can we say anything about the character of the manuscript which Lactantius had or about his method of quoting from it?

Some quotations are free summaries or adaptations, often put into oratio obliqua (1.11.40, 1.12.9, 2.9.12). Some are too brief to offer any significant clues (1.10.2, 3.20.15). Others offer no

---

[13] *De Natura Deorum*, ed. A. S. Pease, p. 55; F. Fessler, *Benutzung d. phil. Schrift. Cic. durch Lactanz* (1903).

[14] For Augustine and his text of the *N.D.* see A. Souter, *C.R.* 14 (1900), 264.

[15] See Pease's note on 3.65 with bibliography.

[16] Reynolds and Wilson, *Scribes and Scholars*, p. 43.

departures from the text transmitted by the manuscripts (2.5.9, 1.11.48). But there remain some where the differences are interesting and important.

Although Lactantius must have had access to a copy of the *N.D.* when he was writing, something of his own fulsome rhetoric seems to have coloured his transcription of certain texts. Thus the correct 'hinc Hercules, hinc Castor et Pollux, hinc Aesculapius . . .' (*N.D.* 2.62) is improved to '. . . hinc Castor, hinc Pollux . . .' *D.I.* 1.15.5) without regard to the fact that Castor and Pollux were thought of as a single unit (cf. *N.D.* 2.6). So too a superfluous *aut* is added to *N.D.* 3.50 ( = *D.I.* 1.15.6) and a superfluous *in* to *N.D.* 2.54 (*in tam variis* = *D.I.* 2.5.8). But the most noticeable feature is the habit of rearranging the word-order, even in defiance of a well-marked clausula, to bring the verb to the end of the clause: for instance, 'necesse est regi' becomes 'regi est necesse' (1.5.24) and 'accipere debeo religionis' 'religionis accipere debeo' (2.6.8).[17] There are also places where Lactantius has simply made mistakes either through carelessness or errors in his copy of the *N.D.* (unless the text of Lactantius itself has been subsequently corrupted); for example, 'appellati ⟨quod nomen patuit postes latius Cic.⟩' (homoeoteleuton), '⟨diligenter Cic.⟩ retractarent', 'his enim ⟨in Cic.⟩ verbis omnibus inest vis' (4.28.5), 'ac (et Cic.) fictos' (1.17.2), 'esse (inesse Cic.)' (2.5.8), 'possem (possim Cic.)' (2.3.24), 'acuendae' (cf. Val. Max. 2.9.9, 7.3.5; Florus 1.2.5; Amm. Marc. 24.2.5: augendae Cic.) (1.15.6),[18] 'facilius (citius Cic.: cf. *Tusc. Disp.* 2.46; *Phil.* 2.25: Lact. is in Or. Obl.)'. A particularly interesting example is 1.17.2 ( = *N.D.* 2.70) where Cicero wrote 'videtisne igitur ut . . . tracta ratio sit' which is altered to '. . . tracta ratio est'. *Videsne ut* etc., with the subjunctive, is the elevated construction (cf. Horace, *Odes* 1.9.1 with Hubbard and Nisbet's note), whereas the use of the indicative is more colloquial (cf. Catullus 61.77 with Fordyce's note). Lactantius is again normalizing.

But there are other places where Lactantius demonstrably preserves a better text. Thus at 2.64 ( = *D.I.* 1.12.4) Lactantius

---

[17] The tendency of scribes to change the word-order of Cicero's speeches in this way is fully documented by W. Rönsch, *Cur et Quomodo Librarii . . . Commutaverint* (Diss. Leipzig, 1914), 8 ff.

[18] But see T. Wopkens, *Advers. Crit.* 1 (1828), 124, who thinks the alteration deliberate.

alone, apart from a conjecture in a late manuscript of the *N.D.*, reads *caelestem* where the Ciceronian archetype Q had *caelest-(i)um*; at 3.6 ( = *D.I.* 2.6.8) Lactantius had the superior readings 'nunc ego intellegam quid tu sentias' for 'nunc ergo intellegam tu quid sentias';[19] at 3.53 ( = *D.I.* 1.6.2) Lactantius gives the correct transliteration Thoyth for the corrupt Theyn or Theyr in Cicero and has 'in Aegyptum profugisse' for 'Aegyptum profugisse' of Q, although elsewhere Cicero always has *in Aegyptum* (cf. *ad Att.* 9.19.3, *in Pis.* 49).

These facts may help us to restore the text of the deeply corrupt passage at 2.71 ( = *D.I.* 4.28.4) which is also referred to by Isidore (*Etym.* 10.234, hardly from Lactantius himself). It is difficult to reconstruct Q from the apparatus of Ax and Pease but it seems to have read 'ut elegantes ex eligendo, tanquam legendo delegendis ex intellegendo intellegentes'. Lactantius has 'tamquam ex eligendo elegantes, ex diligendo diligentes, ex intellegendo intellegentes', as does Isidore apart from 'elegentes'. The reading, which makes perfectly good sense, seems to confirm both *tamquam* (in itself unobjectionable despite 'tamquam relegerent' shortly before) and the unvaried word-order of the three examples cited as comparisons.[20] Lactantius' text is notably freer of major errors than Q and should be retained here too. And at *D.I.* 2.3.2 and 2.18.10–11 (as well as perhaps *De Ira* 13) it preserves invaluable fragments of the lost portions of Book 3 of the *N.D.*

The *De Senectute* (*Cato maior*) was certainly familiar to Lactantius.[21] There are a number of general borrowings from it in Book 7 of the *D.I.* but there is only one extensive quotation (6.20.4–5 = 40). Some scholars, such as Heumann and Heusinger, did indeed think the passage in question to be a later interpolation but that rash conjecture is now rightly forgotten. Lactantius' text shows three variations from the Ciceronian tradition, all of which are to be explained by careless recollection (omission of *tale, esse, omnino*), but it is noteworthy that he has the correct *excitari* which was corrupted by a later branch of the Ciceronian transmission (LAK) into *exercitari*, a word not used in this way by Cicero himself.

---

[19] Ax accepts the manuscript text.
[20] T. Forchammer, *Nordisk tidskrift for filologi* 5 (1880), 51.
[21] P. Wuilleumier, *Mélanges Ernout*, 383 ff.

The *De Divinatione*, which is a natural pendant to the *De Natura Deorum*, had a different fortune in antiquity. Perhaps because it was too sceptical even for the Christians and too abstruse even for the pagans it was very little studied. Valerius Maximus used it as a quarry for examples, Plutarch and Aulus Gellius refer to it. Of the Apologists, Minucius Felix and Arnobius knew it but the only Christian to make extensive use of it was Augustine. It is against this background that we must judge the citations alleged by Brandt. On inspection, it turns out that although Lactantius was aware of the work, he has no verbatim quotations at all. *D.I.* 4.15.27 is just a reference to those who have read Cicero and Varro on the Erythraean Sibyl ( = *De Div.* 1.34); *D.I.* 7.14.14 alludes to 1.36—the claim of the Chaldeans that there were monuments dating back 470,000 years. And that is all. *D.I.* 3.14.13 is not an echo of 2.1, and three lines of Cicero's *De Consulatu* (3.17.14) do not come from the *De Divinatione* (1.19, 2.45) and Lactantius does not claim that they do (see p. 18). The *De Divinatione* will not have been one of Lactantius' working texts.

By contrast the *De Officiis* is almost too familiar. It is quoted with great frequency and inaccuracy, suggesting that Lactantius relied much on his memory. That he himself was aware of this is suggested by the fact that in the second edition of the *D.I.* (as represented by the manuscript R) he makes a number of corrections. Even so we can say something about the text which he must have originally had. Our manuscripts fall into two main classes:

1) Z, represented by the fragmentary Q (Parisinus 6347: 9th c.), B (Bambergensis MVI: 9th–10th c.), V (Vossianus Q 71: 9th–10th c.), and P (Parisinus 6601: 9th–10th c.); 2) X, represented by L (Harleianus 2716: 9th–10th c.), c (Bernensis 104: 12th c.), p (Palatinus 1531: 13th c.). Both branches derive from a common archetype, but the division into two traditions was already in existence by the time of Nonius.[22] Atzert claims that Lactantius' evidence is not informative but in fact it is very similar to Nonius, containing a number of distinctive readings from the X tradition.

The subject-matter was, of course, directly relevant to the sixth book of the *D.I.* (*De Vero Cultu*) from which the bulk of the

[22] Cicero, *De Divinatione*, ed. Atzert (Teubner), pp. xviii–xix.

quotations come. Some of them are precise, and show no variation from the text that has been handed down to us in the
manuscripts (6.11.2, 6.11.9, 6.24.7); some are very general
paraphrases or summaries, often in reported speech (6.5.4,
6.12.11, 3.13.10). Others show simple carelessness (3.13.11
*nam si, est ars, isto*; 3.29.4 *esse fortunae vim, nesciat, pervenimus,
respiravit*;[23] 6.17.27 *potest esse*; 6.11.11 om. *est, egentibus*; 6.6.21
*dirimunt hi*; 6.24.18 *habere*; 6.6.25 *easque, ab*). In yet other
passages Lactantius corrects the text between the two editions
of the *D.I.* (3.13.11 *inquirunt* B: *adquirunt R: anquirunt* Z; 3.29.4
*et* B Cic.: om. R; 6.6.21 *generis humani* B: *humani generis* R Cic.;
6.11.11 *refutandum* B: *repudiandum* R Cic.; 6.6.26–7 *aut Aristides
. . . ab illis* B: [*aut*] *Aristides . . . ab illo* R; *habentur et nominantur* B:
*habiti et nominati* R Cic.). But in a very few places the influence
of the X tradition of Cicero cannot be overlooked (6.12.15 *hanc
ego* Lact. c: *hanc ergo* Z; *longe* Lact. c.: om. Z; 6.12.5 *domus* BZ:
*domos* RX; 6.18.15 *si quis* Lact. p: *si qui* Z; 3.13.10 *inquirunt* Bc
(see above)).

Finally the *Tusculan Disputations*. Lactantius knew all five
books and makes wide use of them (7.10.10, 3.14.7).[24] Cicero
incorporated much of the *Consolatio* in them and it is not always
clear which work Lactantius is actually using (cf. 7.8.9), particularly when he adapts a passage to his own language and
syntax (e.g. 7.8.7).[25] Like so many other of the philosophical
dialogues, the *Tusc. Disp.* survived through an archetype of the
late fifth century, which sired two traditions:

　1) X, represented by R (Parisinus Regius 6332: 9th c.), K
　(Cameracensis: 9th c.) and V (Vaticanus 3246: 9th c.) and

　2) Y, represented by corrections in V and by some Renais-
　sance manuscripts.

Most of Lactantius' quotations show no departures from the
archetypal text (7.8.9 = 1.23, 3.14.8 = 5.6, 7.2.10 = 1.99, 7.10.9
= 1.110, 3.25.2 = 2.4, 3.28.20 = 3.69), apart from minor editorial
adjustments. He does display his usual tendency to normalize
(3.15.9 'alios gloriae' for 'gloriae nonnullos') and to simplify

---

[23] Atzert's app. crit. is wrong.
[24] Brandt attributes 7.8.5 to the *Consolatio* or the *Tusc. Disp.*—without warrant.
[25] One instance (3.19.13) is discussed by M. Hubbard, *Proc. Camb. Phil. Soc.*
201 (1975), 56–7.

(3.15.9 om. *suam*; 3.13.15 om. *vitae*) but in the few significant variations it is worth noting that he has a number of readings which are peculiar to the Y tradition (e.g. 3.13.15 *expultrix*; 3.15.9 *ipse suis*; 1.15.24 *a nobis*), a phenomenon which encourages us to believe that, even despite mistakes (e.g. 1.15.25 'quare quoniam' for 'quaere quorum'), his text is sounder than the archetype. But then this could have been expected.

Perhaps the main point is the gaps in Lactantius' reading. There is not a single reference to the *De Finibus*, the *Paradoxa*, the *De Amicitia*, or the *De Fato*—an astonishing and revealing omission.

## The Speeches

Rhetorical education entailed familiarity with the great speeches of the past, especially those of Cicero, and with the elaborate treatises which set out the principles of the art of speaking. As a professional rhetor Lactantius must have been brought up in that discipline but his own writing betrays remarkably little knowledge of Cicero's oratorical works. There is one very loose allusion to the *Orator* (18 = *D.I.* 3.14.11) but none to the *Brutus*, *De Oratore*, *De Inventione*, or other writings. As for the speeches his range is again surprisingly limited. Brandt detected echoes of the *Pro Deiotaro* (26; cf. *D.I.* 5.6.12 'regias laudes'), the *Philippics* (3.16 = *D.I.* 3.23.7 Tuditanus), and the *Pro Milone* (73 = 1.10.14 the sister of P. Clodius) but the reverberations are infinitely remote. The chief borrowings, apart from a long passage of the Catilinarian (4.12) in the *De Ira* (17.9), come from the Verrines; he knew the complete work, for he not only quotes from the individual books (*Div. in Caec.* 3 = *D.I.* 2.4.31; *Verr.* 2.8 = 1.11.32; 5.35 = 6.24.20), but he gives summaries of the general argument which betray detailed acquaintance (1.10.14, 1.11.32, 3.17.13, 2.4.27–9, 4.18.10). None of those passages, however, throws any light on the text which Lactantius must have known.

The remaining echoes are only four in number and each one is celebrated in its own right and could, therefore, be known independently of the complete speech. Thus *D.I.* 6.18.34 ('spero te inquit Caesari qui oblivisci nihil soles nisi iniurias' = *Pro Lig.* 35) is also found in Quintilian 6.3.108 and Augustine, *Epist.* 138.9. The lapidary 'bene habet, iacta sunt fundamenta'

$(7.1.1 = Pro\ Mur.\ 14)$ was a standard expression of transition (Firm. *Math.* 1.7.1, 5 Praef. 1).

The *Pro Marcello* was the most popular of all the Caesarian speeches[26] and the two quotations which Lactantius makes from it are both found elsewhere: *D.I.* $1.9.4 = Pro\ Marc.$ 8 'animum vincere, iracundiam cohibere...iudico' (cf. Arusianus 7.512 K.) and $6.11.25 = Pro\ Marc.$ 11 'nihil est enim...cottidie magis' (cf. $\Sigma$ Lucan 6.20). It is, however, of note that Lactantius clearly sides with the $\alpha$ branch of the Ciceronian manuscript tradition rather than the $\beta$ (*faciat* $\alpha$Lact: *facit* $\beta$; *lenitas* $\alpha$Lact.: *lenitas animi* $\beta$; *florescet* $\alpha$Lact.: *florescit* $\beta$) which may indicate direct familiarity with a copy of the speech. If so, it is the only speech that we can confidently say that Lactantius had scrutinized, apart from the Verrines and the Catilinarians.[27]

---

[26] G. Kennedy, *The Art of Rhetoric in the Roman World*, 259–60. The popularity of the Catilinarian speeches in Gallic education is illustrated by the fourth-century statuette of a teacher holding a book inscribed with the opening lines of the *First Catilinarian* (*J.R.S.* 66 (1976), 196).

[27] *D.I.* 4.1.1 bears some resemblance to the opening of *De Oratore* but it is traditional; see T. Janson, *Latin Prose Prefaces* (Uppsala, 1964), 156.

# VII.  Seneca

SENECA exerted a great fascination over Christian writers. Tertullian indeed regarded him as *naturaliter Christianus* and a correspondence between him and St. Paul had already been fabricated by the fourth century.[1] The seeds of this idea are in Lactantius also (*D.I.* 6.24.14) when he says that Seneca 'potuit esse verus dei cultor si quis illi monstrasset'. Seneca was indeed the Roman pagan who came closest to the Christian ideal and it was natural that apologists should draw support and ammunition for their cause from him. Tertullian, Minucius, Cyprian, and Clement had all appealed to Seneca, as Augustine and Jerome were to do later. The odd thing, however, about Lactantius is the works of Seneca that he appears to have known.[2] Brandt gives cross-references to the *De Vita Beata* (3.11.6), *De Beneficiis* (6.10.10), and *De Providentia* (3.24.16) but in no case does Lactantius name Seneca and the similarities are extremely general and remote; they are philosophical commonplaces. Of the extant works the *De Ira* is used, not unnaturally, for it is the model for the *De Ira Dei*, and also, once, the *De Providentia*. As Monat has confirmed in his commentary on 5.22.11–12,[3] the allusion which Lactantius makes to the work 'cui titulus est Quare bonis viris multa mala accidant cum sit providentia' is a free paraphrase of several parts of the *De Providentia*. It does not exactly correspond to any one single passage, nor is there any need to assume that it comes from a missing portion of that work.

Lactantius quotes extensively from only three works, the *Exhortationes*, the *De Immatura Morte*, and *Moralis Philosophiae Libri*. No other classical or patristic author refers to them, apart from Seneca himself who in three letters (106.2, 108.39, 109.14, 17) refers to the progress and completion of the Moral

---

[1] A. Momigliano, *R.S.I.* 62 (1950), 325–44; L. Alfonsi, *Athenaeum* 43 (1976), 175, on 'Christian' ideas in Seneca, *Epist.* 73.16.

[2] M. Spannuet, *Rec. Theol.* 31 (1964), 32–42.

[3] Monat gives a full bibliography.

Philosophy. The passages which have been thought to belong
to other works have been in recent years properly placed.[4]
The long historical fragment (7.15.14) which was at one time
thought to come from a projected historical work by Seneca's
father has now been conclusively attributed to Seneca himself
and to the *Exhortationes*.[5]

The initial reaction, which would be to regard these works as
spurious, is unjustifiable. The language and style of the fragments, even when paraphrased by Lactantius, are distinctively
Senecan, as Lausberg has amply demonstrated. It is, therefore,
necessary to examine them more closely.

The *De Immatura Morte* is a puzzle. In the first place only two
quotations (frs. 26, 27 Haase) definitely are attributed to it.
Fragment 29 (*D.I.* 5.13.20 'summa virtus illis videtur magnus
animus et idem eum qui contemnit mortem pro furioso habent
. . .') is merely attributed to Seneca but, as Cellarius pointed
out, the same passage is echoed by Tertullian, *Apol.* 50 discussing examples of endurance to death (cf. 50.11 'si pro deo
patiatur, insanus est'). Tertullian quotes as his authorities
Cicero's *Tusc.Disp.*, Diogenes, Pyrrho, Callinicus, and Seneca
*in Fortuitis*. That work, more fully the *De Remediis Fortuitorum*,
provided answers to objections based on the fear of death. The
resemblance between *D.I.* 5.13 and Tertullian, *Apol.* 50 does,
however, go deeper. The theme was a stock one and is also
covered by Minucius (37.1–6), and the same examples, Mucius,
Regulus and the like (see p. 43), are paraded by all three
authors. It may be, therefore, that Lactantius is working up an
inherited passage, complete with the Seneca quotation. On the
other hand Lausberg (p. 194) points out that Lactantius nowhere mentions the *De Remediis*, and argues that the fragment
should belong to the *Moral Philosphy*.

Fragment 28 ('post mortem omnia finiuntur, etiam ipsa')
quoted three times by Tertullian (*De Anima* 42; *De Resurr.
Carnis* 1.4, 3.3) has been thought to be a paraphrase of *Troades*

---

[4] Notably M. Lausberg, *Untersuchungen zu Senecas Fragmenten* (1970), reviewed by
M. Winterbottom, *C.R.* 22 (1972), 226–8.

[5] M. T. Griffin, *J.R.S.* 62 (1972), 19: *Seneca: a philosopher in Politics* (Oxford,
1976), 194–7, showing how the views on history expressed there agree with others
known to have been held by Seneca. The *De Superstitione*, which was popular in
late antiquity, may be behind 5.20.7 (cf. fr. 34 'dii autem nullo debent coli genere
si et hoc volunt': see Lausberg p. 199) but direct dependence is not necessary.

397 'post mortem nihil est ipsaque mors nihil' but it is significant that Tertullian quotes it always in the same form and that,
in that form, it says something rather different from the
*Troades* line, not that death is nothing but that death too is
finished after death. But that does not prove that it comes from
*De Immatura Morte*, which Tertullian does not quote; it could
be from the *De Remediis*, which he does.

Fragments 26 and 27 certainly are Senecan in language and
thought, as Lausberg shows (pp. 155–63).[6] Yet, there are
misgivings.

In the first place there does not seem to have been a tradition
of writing works on Untimely Death. On Death, certainly:
Philodemus was credited with a Περὶ θανάτου in four books,[7]
and Stobaeus devoted chapter 118 of his *Florilegium* to the
topic; Crantor's Περὶ πένθους may be the inspiration. Given
the traditional nature of philosophical treatises, it would be
surprising if Seneca alone had ventured to devote a whole book
to it,[8] particularly since one section of the *De Remedis Fortuitorum*
is concerned with the objection 'iuvenis morieris'. Untimely
death[9] is usually included among other subjects (cf. Marc. Aur.
*Med.* 2.12, 3.7, 9.3).[10]

Secondly, the context of both fragments is revealing. *D.I.*
1.5 is a list of philosophical views on the nature of the gods. It
forms part of a traditional *theologia tripertita* going back to Varro
and Panaetius, by which the views of poets, philosophers, and
prophets are summarized in three categories. Lactantius quotes
ten Greek philosophers, ending with Cicero and Seneca. Minucius (19) and Cicero (*De Nat. Deorum* 1.37) give a similar list of
Greek philosophers and summarize their views on the same
subject in identical terms. The only difference is that Minucius
quotes an additional eleven philosophers and Cicero an additional seventeen. *D.I.* 3.12 is a more extended survey of definitions of the Supreme Good which harks back to Cicero, *Ac.
Prior.* 2.129 ff. (Euclides, Stoici, Epicurus), but quotes fewer

[6] See also G. Maurach, *Der Bau von Senecas Epistulae Morales* (Heidelberg, 1970),
103, 165–7.
[7] Premature death is handled in coll. 12–20. Bibliography in Lausberg p. 153
nn. 3, 4.
[8] But as M. T. Griffin points out (*Seneca*, 149), Seneca was original in styling
a work *De Clementia* for which there is equally no exact Greek parallel.
[9] 'In eo libro quem de immatura morte conscripsit' (*D.I.* 3.12.11).
[10] R. Kassel, *Untersuchungen zur Konsolationenliteratur* (1958), 80–5.

philosophical schools. Since Lactantius must therefore have found both lists with their quotations in an earlier source, he either found the Seneca quotations already in that source or added them from an anthology which grouped quotations under headings such as *De Immatura Morte*. In that case Lactantius or his source will have wrongly assumed that Seneca had actually written a separate treatise under that title, or wrongly distinguished a section of the *De Remediis*.

The Moral Philosophy was composed towards the very end of Seneca's life. Lactantius quotes from it by title at 1.16.10, 2.2.14, and 6.17.28 and by implication once elsewhere. The quotations are spread over the whole compass of the *D.I.* and there is nothing to suggest that it was not a work which Lactantius knew at first hand. But no other author alludes to it,[11] perhaps because later antiquity was more interested in practical rather than theoretical philosophy. Drawing on the model of Hierocles' Ἠθικὴ Στοιχείωσις, it seems to have been concerned with the fundamentals of ethics—*bonum, sapiens, virtus*, and the emotions. The surviving fragments, discussed fully by Lausberg, give us some indication of its scope.

Fragment 119 attacks in specifically Roman terms (*Lex Papia, Ius trium liberorum*) the poetical myths of Juppiter as an indiscriminate father and asks sarcastically why he has stopped siring children. The topic was a favourite one among pagan and Christian writers alike (Pliny, *N.H.* 2.17; Juvenal 6.58-9; Min. Fel. 24.3; Theophil. *Ad Autol.* 2.3) and Lactantius is embroidering on an apologetic theme which he may have taken over from Theophilus. Fragment 124 discusses the truly wise man, who cares nothing about the trappings of power (cf. *Thyestes* 344 ff.) nor about pain and suffering ('non quaerit quid patiatur sed quam bene': cf. *De Provid.* 2.4). Fragment 120 deals with the stupidity of men who worship idols and not the makers of idols. With this fragment should go an unplaced citation of Seneca (fr. 121 = *D.I.* 2.4.14; on the stupidity of the old, an extension of the proverb δὶς παῖδες οἱ γέροντες) and also, perhaps, the Lucilius quotation of the stupidity of idol-worshippers (see p. 8), but the unplaced fragment 29 more probably comes at second hand from the *De Remediis* and not

---

[11] Lausberg, p. 175 n. 28. Fr. 123 (which is not attributed to a particular work) probably comes from the *Exhortationes*: see p. 77.

from the *Moral Philosophy*, as Lausberg argued (p. 193; see p. 74), and fragment 123 comes from the *Exhortationes*.

Four fragments are little enough to build on, but with the *Exhortationes* we are more fortunate. It clearly owed much to other Protreptici, in particular Cicero's *Hortensius*, but differed from that work in that it advocated a positive rather than contemplative end in life and was not in a dialogue form.[12] The *Hortensius* enjoyed great repute in antiquity (see p. 58) and Seneca's work certainly survived the end of the classical era. It was, it seems, known to Minucius (35.6: see Lausberg on fr. 14) and also Merobaudes and Vincent, the author of the Ps.-Ambrosian *De Paenitentia*. Lactantius evidently knew the whole work. He quotes from the beginning (6.24.16 'eiusdem operis primo') and the close (6.24.12 'exhortationes suas Seneca mirabili sententia terminavit'). The latter passage echoes the former (note *nihil prodest . . . conscientiam*), a kind of ring-composition which Seneca uses elsewhere (e.g. *De Benef.* 1.1.2 and 7.32), and which also serves to underline the theme of the whole work. Lausberg has examined the fragments, and shown how extensive Seneca's coverage was. We may assume that it was a primary source for Lactantius. At times he may be quoting or paraphrasing from memory. Much of *D.I.* 3.25 goes back to the *Exhortationes*, not only the explicit quotation at 3.25.16 ( =fr. 23) on the availability of philosophy to all.[13] In language and context the argument is Senecan but it contains a significant mistake which Seneca could not have made. As the sole example of a slave who took to philosophy 'Pythagoras' is named, instead of the famous Phaedo (Aul. Gell. 2.18). This is a confusion with Pythagoras' slave Zalmoxis who is numbered, along with Persaeus and Epictetus, among those who were encouraged to take up philosophy (Orig. *C. Cels.* 3.24).

---

[12] Lausberg, pp. 56–8, against P. Hartlich, *Leip. Studien* 11 (1899), 306, pointing out that it is Lactantius' habit to name the speaker when quoting from a dialogue.
[13] Lausberg, pp. 127 ff.

# VIII.   The Greek Philosophers

LACTANTIUS lived at a time when Platonism was enjoying its most vigorous revival and when its conflict with Christianity was at its most intellectually intense. Plotinus and Porphyry were both dead, but their works were held in great esteem and their successors continued their tradition. He himself was acquainted with the debate, and devotes a section of Book 5 (5.2) to an attack on Hierocles and another pagan philosopher. But how well did he know the original writings which gave the inspiration to the neo-Platonists?[1]

There are many references to Plato and they repay careful investigation. *D.I.* 3.21 contains a brief summary of Socrates' philosophy which is based on the *Republic* (especially 416 D, 457 C, 463 C, 473 D). The source of it is made clear when Lactantius writes in the corresponding chapter of the *Epitome* 33.1: 'Plato quem deum philosophiae Tullius nominat'. It is Cicero's *Republic*, not Plato's, which Lactantius is using, and the confirmation comes from a chance quotation from Book 4 by the grammarian Nonius (574 L.) which corresponds to *D.I.* 3.21.2. The only allusion to the Platonic Republic is the commonplace that the human figure is god-like (θεοειδής: *D.I.* 2.10.4). Cicero is again the immediate source of several other Platonic passages, e.g. 7.8.4 ( = *Phaedrus* 245 C) comes from *Tusc. Disp.* 1.53–4; 6.25.1 ( = *Laws* 956 A) from *De Leg.* 2.45; *De Ira* 11.13 ( = *Laws* 821 A) from *N.D.* 1.30; 7.22.19 ( = *Phaedo* 72 E, on *anamnesis*) from *Cato* 78; 7.12.2 ( = *Phaedo* 80 D, on the soul) from *Tusc. Disp.* 1.66; 7.2.10 ( = *Apol.* 42 A) explicitly from *Tusc. Disp.* 1.99; *Epit.* 35.5 and *De Ira* 1.7 from *Ac. Prior.* 2.74.

A direct intermediary can be proved in other cases. Thus the quotation from *Phaedo* 60 B in *Epit.* 24.9 occurs in the long passage of Aulus Gellius' *Noctes Atticae* (see p. 46). The passing reference to the *Cratylus* (398 B) has been examined above (p. 20). The saying from *Laws* 934 A 'nemo prudens punit . . .'

---

[1] Pichon, pp. 88 ff.

(*De Ira* 18.5) is evidently taken from Seneca's *De Ira* 1.19. Minucius Felix in this as in other fields proved a convenient quarry. In his long discussion of devils (2.14.9–14) Lactantius makes use of Plato's treatment in the *Symposium* (202 E ff.), but so had Minucius (26.8 ff.) and a comparison of the texts shows that Lactantius has simply adapted what he found in Minucius (p. 93).

Minucius must also be the origin of Lactantius' reference to the *Timaeus* (1.8.1; cf. *De Ira* 11.5 = *Tim.* 28 C: 'dei cuius vim maiestatemque tantam esse dicit in Timaeo Plato ut eam neque mente concipere neque verbis enarrare quisquam possit ob nimiam et inaestimabilem potestatem').[2] Minucius (19.14) paraphrases the same passage but his version is much closer to Plato. Lactantius' language (cf. 'mente concipere', 'inaestimabilis') shows that he has adapted Minucius in his own words. The sentence from the *Timaeus* was in any case much quoted in Apologetic (cf. Tertullian, *Apol.* 46.9; see Beaujeu's note on Minucius ad loc.).

But the *Timaeus* reference does raise a complicated issue. In the *Epitome* (64.5) Lactantius gives a much fuller version of this section, which has nothing corresponding to it in the *D.I.* Similarly in *Epit.* 63. 1–5 he paraphrases *Tim.* 29 E and in 63.9 *Tim.* 42 B and 90 E: neither is reflected in the *D.I.* itself. Therefore, just as between writing the *D.I.* and the *Epitome* he seems to have discovered Aulus Gellius (p. 47), so he must have extended his reading in philosophy. This fact may be connected with the widespread interest which the *Timaeus* seems to have aroused in the West during this age and which led to Chalcidius' translation and commentary. Chalcidius' date is uncertain, but in any case Lactantius is not using his translation (cf. *Epit.* 63.1 'quia bonus est et invidens nulli, fecit quae bona sunt' ~ *Tim.* 29 E 'optimus erat, ab optimo porro invidia longe relegata est. Itaque consequenter cuncta sua similia . . . effici voluit'). It may be that the publication of the *D.I.* and the *Epitome* encouraged Chalcidius, who was also a Christian, to undertake the task. All we know about Chalcidius is that he made use of Origen and Porphyry among his latest sources and that he

[2] A. Wlosok (*Lactanz*, 202, 226, 252 ff.) postulates a Gnostic-Platonist source grounded in Hermetic speculation. A. D. Nock (*Vig. Chr.* 16 (1962), 79), discussing interpretations of the *Timaeus* passage, rejects Wlosok's argument but does not himself advance any views on the immediate origin of Lactantius' quotations.

dedicated his book to Osius, Bishop of Corduba. A Cordovan bishop of that name presided over the Council of Sardinia in A.D. 343.[3] Greek commentaries on the *Timaeus* were, of course, common during this period and Chalcidius made use both of Porphyry's and Iamblichus'. The *Epitome* is also the first work to show knowledge of the mystical pseudo-Platonic doctrine of the first and second God ( = *Epinomis* 986 C; *Epist.* 6.323 C), but this was a regular feature of Apologetic (Eusebius, *Praep. Evang.* 11.15.7 ff.; Justin, *Apol.* 1.92 E–93 C) and so did not require consultation of the Platonic corpus itself.

This analysis leaves one work from which Lactantius quotes some passages without any obvious intermediary—the *Phaedo*. On inspection that knowledge is more circumscribed. In 7.22.19 he mentions 'Plato de anima disserens' and gives a summary of the theory of *anamnesis* but nothing in it corresponds exactly to a Platonic passage (cf. *Phaedo* 72 E), and the language rather recalls Cicero, *Cato* 78 (note, especially, *rapiant ~ arripiant*), although the parallelism is not quite exact. The quotation from *Phaedo* 60 B (*Epit.* 24.9) comes from Aulus Gellius (see p. 47), and the argument that the soul is weightless (7.12.2 = *Phaedo* 80 D) is close to that put forward by Cicero (*Tusc. Disp.* 1.66). But other passages do not have obvious sources. Even if the definition 'mors est naturae animantium dissolutio' ( = *Phaedo* 64 C [θάνατον εἶναι] τὴν τῆς ψύχης ἀπὸ τοῦ σώματος ἀπαλλαγήν) will have become a commonplace, Lactantius shows familiarity with *Phaedo* 80 C-D:

c    Πῶς γὰρ οὔ;
     Ἐννοεῖς οὖν, ἔφη, ἐπειδὰν ἀποθάνῃ ὁ ἄνθρωπος, τὸ μὲν ὁρατὸν αὐτοῦ, τὸ σῶμα, καὶ ἐν ὁρατῷ κείμενον, ὃ δὴ νεκρὸν καλοῦμεν, ᾧ προσήκει διαλύεσθαι καὶ διαπίπτειν καὶ διαπνεῖσθαι, οὐκ εὐθὺς τούτων οὐδὲν πέπονθεν, ἀλλ' ἐπιεικῶς συχνὸν ἐπιμένει χρόνον, ἐὰν μέν τις καὶ χαριέντως ἔχων τὸ σῶμα τελευτήσῃ καὶ ἐν τοιαύτῃ ὥρᾳ, καὶ πάνυ μάλα· συμπεσὸν γὰρ τὸ σῶμα καὶ ταριχευθέν, ὥσπερ οἱ ἐν Αἰγύπτῳ ταριχευ-
d    θέντες, ὀλίγου ὅλον μένει ἀμήχανον ὅσον χρόνον, ἔνια δὲ μέρη τοῦ σώματος, καὶ ἂν σαπῇ, ὀστᾶ τε καὶ νεῦρα καὶ τὰ τοιαῦτα, πάντα, ὅμως ὡς ἔπος εἰπεῖν ἀθάνατά ἐστιν· ἢ οὔ;

At *D.I.* 7.1.9 he writes 'omne quod sub visum oculorum venit et corporale, ut ait Plato, et solubile sit necesse est', and at 7.12.6

---

[3] De Tamilia, *S.I.F.C.* 8 (1900), 79 ff.; R. Klibansky, *Plato Latinus: Timaeus* (Brill, 1962), i–xvii.

'integrum corpus manet et plerumque medicatum [= ταριχευθέν] diutissime durat'.

If Lactantius had read it in the original, that one passage would have been exceptional. Perhaps he had, for it was deservedly famous (Plutarch seems to allude to it in *Adv. Colotem* 1103 E), but it may well be that he found it in an anthology. Considerable study has been made recently of Platonic quotations in the Fathers and in neo-Platonic writers,[4] and the evidence points towards an anthology which contained extracts from such Dialogues as the *Timaeus, Phaedo, Republic, Laws,* and *Cratylus*. This passage of the *Phaedo* is one such, as is proved by its inclusion in Stobaeus, *Florilegium* 1.49 (p. 330 Wachsmuth), and by its quotation by Eusebius (*Praep. Evang.* 11.27) and Theodoret of Cyr (*Therapeut.* 5.42). In the face of this it would be a bold man who claimed that here alone Lactantius had recourse to Plato himself.

No written source, let alone a text of Plato, is needed for the legend of Pythagoras and Plato visiting Egypt and beyond (4.2.3–5). It is part of the mythology surrounding the revival of Platonism which sought to link it with the wisdom of the East. Plato's journey is mentioned as early as Cicero (*De Rep.* 1.16; *De Fin.* 5.87; cf. Diod. Sic. 1.98; Quintilian 1.12.15; Strabo 17.1.29; Lucan 10. 188 ff.) and his association with Eastern Magi comes first in Philostratus (*Vita Apoll.* 1.2; cf. Diog. Laert. 3.7; Apuleius, *De Plat.* 1.3; Pausanias 4.32.4). Early Christian writers extended Plato's inquiries into the Mosaic law ([Justin], *Cohortatio* 20; Clement, *Protr.* 70.1; Origen, *C. Cels.* 4.39.7). Lactantius is, therefore, merely developing an apologetic commonplace.[5]

Aristotle also was a stranger to him. His name occurs four times but the context of each passage shows that the reference is derivative. In *De Opificio* 12.6 Aristotle is bracketed with Varro, the real ultimate source ('conceptum igitur V. et A. sic fieri arbitrantur. aiunt . . .' = *De Anim. Gener.* 4.3). In *D.I.* 5.14.5 Lactantius deals with Carneades' refutation of Aristotle and Plato, which figured in the third book of Cicero's *Republic*. Aristotle's doctrine (*De Caelo* 1.10) that the world had always existed and will always exist is mentioned twice (2.10.7, 7.1.7),

---

[4] P. Canivet, *Théodoret de Cyr: Thérapeutique* (Sources Chrétiennes 57), 1.57.

[5] H. Dörrie, *Romanitas et Christianitas*, 99 ff.

but it was a familiar doctrine, regularly raised by Cicero (e.g. *Tusc. Disp.* 1.70; *Ac. Prior.* 2.119). Finally the passing reference to man as a social animal is borrowed from Seneca's *De Beneficiis* (7.1.7), as the surrounding arguments show.

Apart from Epicurus, other philosophers are rarely cited. The long list of summaries of philosophical views in 1.5.15–25, part of the *theologia tripertita*, was traditional, perhaps immediately from Seneca (p. 75). Antisthenes on natural and popular gods (fr. 24 = *De Ira* 11.14) is, along with the philosophical excerpts in that chapter, taken as a whole from Cicero, *N.D.* 1.31–2 or Minucius 29.7; Zeno on the λόγος ( = *D.I.* 4.9.2) comes from Tertullian, *Apol.* 21; and Empedocles' four elements were too well known to need documentation (*D.I.* 2.12.4; *De Opif.* 17.6). The location of the soul in the head (*De Opif.* 16.6) is not attributed to Theophrastus by name (cf. *De Sensu* 42) and is not, therefore, directly from him. There is one quotation (in Latin) from Asclepiades, *De Providentia* (*D.I.* 7.4.17). We know nothing of him except that he was a friend of Lactantius, who addressed two books to him (Jerome, *De Viris Ill.* 80). He was presumably a Christian but his name does not demand that he was a Greek. The allusion to Lucian (1.9.8) is a textual interpolation and the mention of Apollonius of Tyana and Apuleius (5.2.7) does not imply acquaintance with their writings. Indeed the distorted picture of Apuleius as a magician suggests, if anything, the reverse. He is similarly linked with Apollonius in Augustine (*Epist.* 136.1, 138.18).

Only Chrysippus is quoted extensively. Apart from a mention in Varro's account of the history of the Sibyls (1.6.9) and the commonplace on mice (*De Ira* 13.10–12; see p. 37), one passage of Chrysippus (*De Prov.* 4 fr. 26) is embedded in the long quotation from Aulus Gellius (see p. 47), another is a reworking of Cicero, *N.D.* 2.16, and a third, the definition of God (1.5.20), is part of the long summary of definitions from Cicero or Minucius (p. 75). Lactantius does, however, cite in Greek one sentence from the *De Providentia*[6] on the possibility of rebirth (7.23.3). He introduces it with a reminiscence of Cicero's *Ac. Prior.* 2.75 where Chrysippus was called the pillar of the

---

[6] Von Arnim (*Stoicorum Veterum Fragmenta* 623) attributes it to the *De Mundo* but Plutarch also quotes from the first book of the *De Providentia* two passages on the renewal of the world (*S.V.F.* 604, 605).

Stoic portico ('fulcire porticum Stoicorum'), but Cicero does not have the quotation, nor, for that matter, does anyone else. The *De Providentia* was a popular work in antiquity, so that it is reasonable that Lactantius should have had access to it. Some of the general references to the Stoici may, as von Arnim thought, come from there (cf. *D.I.* 1.1.2 = *S.V.F.* 1109; *De Ira* 5 = *S.V.F.* 1120; *D.I.* 2.10.5 'Stoici cum de providentia disserunt' = *S.V.F.* 1167), but many of them were traditional doctrines learnt in the schools (e.g. God is formless (*De Ira* 18; cf. Clement, *Strom.* 7.7); God is material (*D.I.* 7.3.1–2; cf. Tertullian, *Apol.* 47)) or reported by authors such as Cicero and Seneca.[7]

---

[7] On Plato and Lactantius see now M. Perrin in *Actes du Colloque de Chantilly* (1977) who reaches very similar conclusions.

# IX.  Epicurus

EPICURUS is named many times and his doctrines subjected to ridicule and contempt, but Epicureanism was so long established and had been taught and attacked in schools for so long that one should be cautious in assuming that Lactantius had read any of the Master's actual works. These, especially the letters and the Κύριαι Δόξαι, did survive, but his teachings were too notorious to need verification by chapter and verse. Indeed it is easy to see how quickly they were distorted and misrepresented, so that it was the travesties of Epicurean views which captured the popular imagination and were passed down. One clear example of this is the proposition ascribed to Epicurus that it is pleasant to be tortured, and that even those in Phalaris' bull will cry out 'suave est et nihil curo' (*D.I.* 3.27.5). This was an old jibe, invented perhaps by Cicero (*In Pis.* 42) and repeated by Seneca (*Epist.* 66.18, 67.15). But Epicurus did not say that torture is pleasurable, he said that one could be 'happy' on the rack, even when screaming and lamenting (Diog. Laert. 10.118; see Nisbet's note on Cic. loc. cit.). Lactantius, therefore, did *not* get this quotation from Epicurus direct. So too the reference to Epicurus' teaching that philosophy was available to all (3.25.4, 7,13 = fr. 227a) is securely embedded in a long section derived from Seneca's *Exhortationes* (see p. 77). Nor is he likely to have got any others directly either. Certainly none is quoted in Greek.

In fact his references to Epicurus (as opposed to Lucretius) fall into two distinct categories—the elaborate refutation of Epicureanism in 3.17 and incidental remarks elsewhere. The latter are either trivial commonplaces or can be shown to be drawn from Lucretius or Cicero. At 3.12.13–16 (cf. *De Ira* 17.1 = fr. 300), for instance, Lactantius says that Epicurus held God to be *beatus* and *incorruptus* because eternally at rest. Yet this is in fact no more than a variation of one of the most famous of all Epicurean dogmas (see the *testimonia* in Usener, e.g. Seneca, *De Benef.* 4.4.1, Tertullian, *Apol.* 47.6, Cicero, *N.D.*

1.85)[1] and one which Lactantius specifically quotes at 5.10.12. At 2.10.24 (cf. 7.1.10 = fr. 304) he mentions the doctrine that the universe was born and will perish. Significantly in mentioning it he brackets Democritus' name with Epicurus, as he does at 2.8.48 and 7.3.23 (see below), thereby showing that he has not had recourse to Epicurus. There again it was familiar Epicurean doctrine [Philo], ἀφθ. κόσμ. 3, also including Democritus; Σ Lucan 7.1). A corollary of this was that Democritus/ Epicurus was unable to explain why the world should be born in the first place (7.3.23 = fr. 382), a failure which generations of teleological thinkers were quick to point out (Aetius 2.3.1; Galen, *De Usu Partium* 11). So too the view that there was no divine Providence (ἀπρονοησία: 1.2.2, 2.8.48–50 = fr. 368) had long been a weapon in the patristic armour (cf. Clement, *Protr.* 5.20.8).

The paradox that the fear of death should drive men to death (2.32.2 = fr. 497) was equally trite, but here the immediate source seems rather to have been Lucretius (3.79–82). Only two other passages need to be noticed. Both involve definitions of the Supreme Good. It is pleasure of the mind (3.7.7 = fr. 452) or absence of pain (3.8.10 = fr. 419). The first is a well-known commonplace (cf. Diog. Laert. 10.137 etc.), the second is attributed to Epicurus by Cicero (*Tusc. Disp.* 3.47; cf. *De Fin.* 2.28) and Plutarch (*Epic. Beat.* 1091b), but by Lactantius, jestingly, to the 'clinici philosophi'—the 'bed-ridden' philosophers who are contrasted with the Peripatetics 'the Walkers' and the Stoics 'the Boulevardiers'. The jest is a turgid and complicated one[2] but it clearly denotes later Epicureans rather than Epicurus himself.

3.17, however, is a concentrated summary of Epicureanism. It is not derived *en bloc* from one source since it contains two quotations from Lucretius (2.1101 ff., 3.1043 ff.; the *poeta inanissimus*), one from Cicero's *Verrines* (4.69) and one from Cicero's poem on his Consulship (cf. *De Div.* 1.19). Neither of these last two is likely to have been utilized by other intermediaries. But it also contains no less than fifteen Epicurean

---

[1] H. Hagendahl, *Latin Fathers and the Classics*, 71, thinks that Cicero was the immediate source.

[2] A. Goulon, *R. E. Aug.* 19 (1973), 39–55, interprets it as philosophers who offer bedside consolation. It is also made by Cyprian (p. 89).

propositions, some of which cannot be easily paralleled elsewhere. Thus the claims that there are no natural bonds towards
parents (fr. 529) and that kingship is a nuisance (fr. 557), or the
praise of solitude (fr. 571; but cf. Diog. Laert. 10.20) are not
enunciated by other authors. But one should not make too
much of this; for it remains certain that the writings of Epicurus himself were not the quarry from which the material
came. In at least one place Lactantius ascribes to Epicurus'
'stupidity' an argument which is nowhere to be found in Epicurus' extant work. This is the question of the hooked atoms
(3.17.23–7). Leucippus had, of course, postulated such a
theory and it recurs in Lucretius (2.387–477), but Usener has
no warrant for identifying an Epicurean fragment here (fr. 287).
It belongs to debased Epicureanism.

  The obvious source would be Cicero's *Hortensius* as Usener
argued and other scholars such as Ruch[3] have held. The *Hortensius* is indeed quoted twice in the preceding chapter (3.16.5,
12)[4] and it is clear that in it Hortensius delivered an attack on
philosophy in general. An independently preserved fragment
of the *Hortensius* (26, in Nonius 674 L.) mentions the school of
Democritus so that it could be argued that Hortensius passed
on from them to the Epicureans. Certainly fr. 13 looks like an
attack on Epicurean cosmology, just as fr. 30 looks like an
attack on Stoic dialectic. Moreover, there are similarities with
other works of Cicero, especially the *De Finibus* (which Lactantius seems not to have known). Thus, the theme of the
popularity of Epicurus is taken up in *De Fin.* 1.25 and of the
Epicurean liking for payment in *De Fin.* 2.30. So too Lactantius' description of Epicurus as a *homo astutus* could echo
Cicero's *homo acutus* (*De Fin.* 1.19). Other arguments also recur
such as that pain is evil (*De Fin.* 2.92), that pleasure justifies
wrongdoing (*De Fin.* 2.56), or the question how atoms coalesce
(*De Fin.* 1.20). But there are some serious objections. Although
Cicero did share the popular view that Epicurean atoms were
hooked (*aduncus*; cf. *N.D.* 1.66), he does not seem to have anti-
cipated the destructive argument which Lactantius uses

---

[3] *L'Hortensius de Cicéron*, 90.
[4] The debt of this chapter of Lactantius to the *Hortensius* is stressed and extended
by C. O. Brink (*J.R.S.* 51 (1961), 217) who shows good reason for thinking that
§§ 11, 13, and 16 are also inspired by Cicero. Also the very important § 9 'philosophi
est quid in vita faciendum vel non faciendum sit disputare'.

against it ('secari ergo ac dividi possunt'), but the use of *ergo* may indicate precisely an addition by Lactantius himself. More telling is the general point that the *Hortensius* is a work designed to encourage philosophical activity and is, therefore, unlikely to have contained particular and detailed attacks on individual schools of philosophy which Cicero would have had to meet and rebuff in order to maintain the credibility of the subject as a whole. O. Gigon,[5] however, is right to remind us that the *Hortensius* is the first of a trilogy comprising the lost *Catulus* and the surviving *Lucullus* and that the more controversial rebuttals could have occurred in the *Catulus* (see above, p. 58). In the *Hortensius* Cicero contented himself with an answer to the general question εἰ φιλοσοφητέον. In fact a detailed rebuttal of the attack on Epicureanism is not necessary and, so far as we know, neither Catulus nor any other of the interlocutors was an Epicurean.

Another candidate would be Seneca. We have seen that some Epicurean material was embedded in his *Exhortationes* (p. 84) and there are Senecan features about the style of the chapter, especially 'alios ... alios ... alios' etc. in 17.8.

[5] *Philologus* 106 (1962), 222 ff.

# X.  The Apologists

OF all the Latin Christians the closest in style and time was Cyprian, Bishop of Carthage, who was martyred in A.D. 258. Lactantius speaks highly of him (5.1.24–8), praising his eloquence and his clarity, but lamenting the fact that he preached only to the converted[1] and therefore did not command the audience that he deserved. His main achievement was the compilation of an anthology of the Latin Bible, which is discussed elsewhere (p. 97), but Cyprian was known not only for his correspondence but for a number of other short and telling monographs. It is not clear, however, how many of these Lactantius used or knew. Certainly the *Ad Demetrianum* whose opening ('oblatrantem et obstrepentem') is echoed in *D.I.* 5.4.3. The same work may, therefore, be the source of Lactantius' scathing arguments against gods who have to be protected by their worshippers rather than protecting them (14 = *D.I.* 2.4.6: note the coincidence of language, e.g. 'tutelam sperare, a colentibus vindicentur'). Other allusions are less sure and none explicit. Thus Lactantius' favourite topic, man's upright stance, does indeed figure prominently in *Ad Dem.* 16, but it is a commonplace, and the denunciation of demons who betray their names under torture (*Ad Dem.* 15) is a standard theme in the apologists.[2]

At first sight it is plausible that Lactantius is borrowing from *Ad Donat.* 8 for his remarks on the theatre (*D.I.* 6.20.27–31). The whole passage is obviously a derivative and literary one,

[1] *Mystica*. See Barnes, *J.T.S.* 25 (1974), 437–9. On Cyprian see U. Koch, *Ric. Rel.* 7 (1931), 122 ff. For Lactantius and Cyprian see P. Monat, *Livre V*, 1.47 with bibliography; R. Weber, *S. Cypriani Episcopi Opera* (Corpus Christianorum 3), 1. XXXIV–V. For Christian diatribes against the games see A. H. M. Jones, *Later Roman Empire*, 3.328; Alan Cameron, *Circus Factions* (Oxford, 1976), 224.

[2] I have listed some passages in my note in *J.T.S.* 76 (1975), 410 ff. I am, however, less certain that the text of *D.I.* 2.15.3 is corrupt. There is a very striking linguistic parallel, which I overlooked, in 2.16.4. 'Veris suis nominibus cient, illis caelestibus quae in litteris sanctis leguntur.' In view of the parallel, I think we must retain the text and interpret 'in templis adorantur' as of the inmost, secret worship by pagan believers. Shackleton Bailey's emendation remains no less unacceptable.

owing little to any personal familiarity with the stage. Both the language and the themes are similar. Comedies deal with the rape of virgins and liaisons with prostitutes, tragedies perpetuate the memories of parricide and incest. Actors are debased by performing lewd and unnatural gestures, *mimi* encourage vice by the popularity of their imitations. Spectators return home corrupted by what they have witnessed and applauded. There are also phrases in common, e.g. 'spectari libenter, de spectaculo revertitur impudica'. But the Lactantius passage needs to be seen in the wider context of chapters 20–4 of the sixth book of the *D.I.* as a whole. As Mai saw, they form a unity and are very close to what we can reconstruct of the argument of the missing fourth book of Cicero's *De Republica*. That might be a more likely source for both Cyprian and Lactantius—and also Minucius Felix (37.11–12) who indulges in a similar tirade.

The *Quod Idola* (13) does bear a very close resemblance to the *D.I.* (4.15.23). The power of Christ to rule the elements is spelled out in specific examples: in Lactantius He could compel 'ventos obsequi, maria servire, morbos cedere, inferos oboedire', in Cyprian 'servire ventos, maria oboedire, inferos cedere'. This looks like a typical case of Lactantius extemporizing from memory. Its subject-matter precludes it from being derived ultimately from some pagan writer. Not even Orpheus did so much.

On the other hand, no weight can be put on Cyprian's allusions in a letter to *clinici* philosophers (*Epist.* 69.16: see p. 85) nor on two possible reminiscences of the *De Opere et Eleemosynis* (9 ~ *D.I.* 6.12.32 the *reductio ad absurdum* that 'if I give all my money to the poor, I shall have no money to give to the poor'; 25 ~ 5.14.16 ff. God gives all alike light, water, food, sleep). The latter commonplace occurs with variations also in *De Bono Patientiae* 4 and *Ad Demetr.* 8 but none of the Cyprianic passages has all four constituents.

But we should not expect Lactantius to have used him widely. It would have been at variance with all his principles. Where he does seem to use him, it is notable that it is for arguments which are far more rhetorical than they are Christian. But then Cyprian, like Lactantius, had been a professor.

Jerome twice asserts that Lactantius was a pupil of Arnobius, the great polemicist from Numidia (*De Viris Illustr.* 80; *Epist.*

70.5) and in such matters Jerome is not likely to have been mistaken. We might therefore, reasonably expect that Lactantius would have listed him among his predecessors as apologists and quoted from his great work, the *Adversus Nationes*, the more so since Arnobius shares with Lactantius a comprehensive acquaintance with Lucretius. Yet, there is no mention of him in the *D.I.*, nor, I suspect, is there even any unacknowledged borrowing. The apparent resemblance between *D.I.* 3.3.2 and *Adv. Nat.* 2.51 (on the interpretation of sense-data) is no more than a stock Epicurean puzzle which is discussed by Lucretius (5.564 ff.), Cicero (*De Fin.* 1.20; *Ac. Post.* 2.82) and other authors. There is nothing peculiarly Arnobian about it or about his treatment of angels and devils (2.24.4: cf. *Adv. Nat.* 2.35). The only clear case of common material is the discussion of Faunus (1.22.9–11) but that comes, indirectly but independently, to both authors from Varro (p. 51). The explanation of this perhaps surprising lack of contact may be that Lactantius had left Africa for Nicomedia before the conversion of Arnobius or at least before the publication of the *Adv. Nat.* which we know to have been very late in his life, perhaps about A.D. 305.

Tertullian (*c.* 170–*c.* 212)[3] he knew and revered, but he found, like many others since, his Latin 'multum obscurus' (5.1.23). Indeed Tertullian's influence was diminished as much by his obscurity as by his heterodoxy. But the *Apologeticum* always held its place as one of the great works of the Church and its effect can be seen in the writings of Minucius Felix and all his successors. That work at least Lactantius knew, even if he did not always understand (5.4.3). But, oddly enough, although there are nearly ten close points of contact with the *D.I.*, none of them compels us to believe that Lactantius was actually recalling the *Apologeticum* or had a copy of it under his eye. Thus *Apol.* 3.5 makes the same point as *D.I.* 4.7.5 about the assimilation of Christos to Chrestos, but does not have the further analogy of the purple and the unction as signs of kingship. *Apol.* 14.4 (followed exactly by Min. Felix 24.5) gives a clearer and more accurate history of Apollo and Neptune. *D.I.* 1.10.3 deals with the same subject-matter but confuses the issues by identifying Apollo and Neptune as the builders of the Trojan Walls. This could be carelessness but Lactantius adds

---

[3] T. D. Barnes, *Tertullian*, 58–9; P. Monat, *Livre V*, 1.45 with bibliography.

an extra story of the beautiful boy killed by Apollo. In the same way *Apol.* 23 looks very like *D.I.* 4.27 (on gods and demons) at first sight; yet there is a sentence in *D.I.* (4.27.11 'si sunt aliqua ... [non] miscebimus'),[4] which is integral to the whole of his argument, that has no equivalent in Tertullian. The common treatment of λόγος–*verbum*–*sermo* in *Apol.* 21.12 and *D.I.* 1.8.6 no doubt occurred in much apologetic, as did Socrates and Aesculapius' cock (46.5 ∼ 3.20.16).

One epigram does look borrowed (*Apol.* 24.6 'ut non liceat mihi colere quem velim sed cogar colere quem nolim' = *D.I.* 5.13.18)—and such epigrams are what one might expect Lactantius to have remembered and stored up. If he really utilized the *Apologeticum* as a working text, the proof of it might have been at 1.23.2, the historian Thallus' account of Belus and the chronology of the Trojan War which occurs in the Fuldensis version of the *Apol.* (19) but not in the surviving tradition. The relation of the Fuldensis to the other manuscripts has recently been reconsidered by Barnes who suggests (pp. 239–41) that so far from there being two independent recensions of the work by Tertullian himself, represented in the Fuldensis and the remaining manuscripts, there was a heavily annotated and contaminated text circulating in the fourth century and used by such authors as Jerome, Rufinus, and the author of the *Quod Idola*. Alas, Lactantius throws no light on this fascinating question, because he expressly cites Theophilus, *Ad Autolycum*, as his source (see p. 38) and it is certain that it is indeed Theophilus and not Tertullian that he is using.

The *Apologeticum* dates from about A.D. 197 and many of its themes are taken up in later works. Thus in the *Ad Praxean* (5.7) of *c.* 210 he reiterates views about the Word and about angels which he had put forward in *Apol.* 21, but there is no suggestion of Lactantius having used it. The *Ad Scapulam*, however, Tertullian's last work of 212, foreshadows the *De Mortibus Persecutorum* in its subject-matter and tone. We might expect some reference to it, but the overlaps are of the most general kind (e.g. 3 = *D.I.* 5.23.1: the guilty will not get off unpunished), and there is no specific allusion to it. Other works, which would have been very relevant to some of the central issues of the *D.I.*,

---

[4] Shackleton Bailey (*Vig. Chris.* 14 (1960), 168) is clearly right about the text.

such as the *De Spectaculis* or the *De Anima*, appear to have been quite unknown to him.

Theophilus, Bishop of Antioch, was a close contemporary of Tertullian's. Jerome says he became Bishop in A.D. 169 and he refers, in his apologetic work to Autolycus (3.28),[5] to the death of Marcus Aurelius (A.D. 180). This work quickly established itself as a popular tract. It was used almost at once by Tertullian and by Irenaeus. In the third century both Novatian (*De Trinitate*) and Methodius referred to it. So it had a settled place in the theological armoury of the Latin West, perhaps because it was so unequivocally monotheistic, or perhaps because it was simple, direct, and comprehensible. Even so it is remarkable that this is the only Greek theological work to which Lactantius refers (1.23.2), indeed the only one that he can be shown to have utilized. Justin, Clement, Origen, Hippolytus—none of the great writers figures in the *D.I.* Yet Lactantius' choice is understandable enough. Not only was Theophilus accepted reading in Christian Africa but he shared with Lactantius certain common interests—in the Sibylline Oracles (p. 28) and in Jewish Christianity (p. 106)—and, during his contact at Nicomedia with Hellenistic Christians, Lactantius will have come across their basic texts. I have argued above (p. 30) that he had a substantially poorer text than that which has survived in our manuscripts; yet even the Belus passage (*D.I.* 1.23.2 = 3.29) is no more than a free summary in oratio obliqua. He adds that the Babylonians, as well as the Assyrians, worship Belus—a detail not in our texts of Theophilus and not likely to have been omitted by manuscript corruption. Lactantius is here again improving on his memory.

Finally, what any dispassionate reader can only regard as the gem of Latin apologetic writing—Minucius Felix's *Octavius*. M. Beaujeu[6] has established beyond doubt that Minucius was inspired by Tertullian's *Apologeticum* and that, therefore, his *Octavius* belongs in the middle of the third century. Lactantius rightly discerned Minucius' potentiality (5.1.21) and regretted only that he had not undertaken any full-scale defence of Christiantiy. But Minucius' style was seductive and his approach congenial to an author of Lactantius' temperament.

[5] Edited by R. M. Grant (Oxford, 1970).
[6] *Octavius*, trans. and commentary (Paris, 1964).

He makes one direct allusion to the *Octavius* (1.11.55 = 21.7: on Saturn) but the debt goes much further. It is, however, difficult to achieve precision, because many of the overlaps involve traditional commonplaces of Apologetic which Lactantius may, or may not, have owed directly to Minucius and also, since Minucius was adapting Tertullian's *Apologeticum*, a work also known to Lactantius, we cannot always be sure which of his two predecessors Lactantius is actually recalling. Brandt lists eighteen borrowings, Beaujeu in his edition of the *Octavius*[7] twenty-three but only six of these actually coincide.

The one specific allusion is 23.12[8] ( = *D.I.* 1.11.55 on Saturn). The same passage names, as historical authorities for Saturn, Nepos, Cassius, Thallus, and Diodorus (23.9) who occur in *D.I.* 1.13.8. Although Minucius has adapted the whole section from Tertullian (*Apol.* 10.7–10), it is reasonable to think that Lactantius is using the more recent writer (p. 38). It is also clear that he is indebted to the *Octavius* for much of his treatment of devils in *D.I.* 2.14–15 as a comparison of the two passages shows.

Philosophi quoque de his disserunt. nam Plato etiam naturas eorum in Symposio exprimere conatus est et Socrates esse circa se adsiduum daemona loquebatur, qui puero sibi adhaesisset, cuius nutu et arbitrio sua vita regeretur. magorum quoque ars omnis ac potentia horum adspirationibus constat, a quibus invocati visus hominum praestigiis obcaecantibus fallunt, ut non videant ea quae sunt et videre se putent illa quae non sunt. hi ut dico spiritus contaminati ac perditi per omnem terram vagantur et in solacium perditionis suae perdendis hominibus operantur. itaque omnia insidiis fraudibus dolis erroribus conplent: adhaerent enim singulis hominibus et omnes ostiatim domos occupant ac sibi geniorum nomen adsumunt; sic enim latino sermone daemonas interpretantur. hos in suis penetralibus consecrant, his cotidie ⟨vina⟩ profundunt, et scientes daemonas venerantur quasi terrestres deos et quasi depulsores malorum quae ipsi faciunt et inrogant. qui quonian spiritus sunt tenues et inconprehensibiles, insinuant se corporibus hominum et occulte in visceribus operati valetudinem vitiant, morbos citant, somniis animos terrent, mentes furoribus quatiunt, ut homines his malis cogant ad eorum auxilia decurrere. (*D.I.* 2.14.9–14)

---

[7] p. cxii.
[8] I follow Beaujeu in keeping to manuscript order of the text of Minucius and rejecting the transpositions often made by editors.

Spiritus sunt insinceri, vagi, a caelesti vigore terrenis labibus et cupiditatibus degravati. isti igitur spiritus, posteaquam simplicitatem substantiae suae onusti et inmersi vitiis perdiderunt, ad solacium calamitatis suae non desinunt perditi iam perdere et depravati errorem pravitatis infundere et alienati a deo inductis pravis religionibus a deo segregare. eos spiritus daemonas esse poetae sciunt, philosophi disserunt, Socrates novit, qui ad nutum et arbitrium adsidentis sibi daemonis vel declinabat negotia vel petebat. Magi quoque non tantum sciunt daemonas sed etiam quicquid miraculi ludunt, per daemonas faciunt: illis adspirantibus et infundentibus praestigias edunt, vel quae non sunt videri, vel quae sunt non videri. eorum magorum et eloquio et negotio primus Hostanes et verum deum merita maiestate prosequitur et angelos, id est ministros et nuntios, dei sedem tueri eiusque venerationi novit adsistere, ut et nutu ipso et vultu domini territi contremescant. idem etiam daemonas prodidit terrenos, vagos, humanitatis inimicos. Quid? Plato, qui invenire deum negotium credidit, nonne et angelos sine negotio narrat et daemonas? et in Symposio etiam suo naturam daemonum exprimere conititur? vult enim esse substantiam inter mortalem inmortalemque, id est inter corpus et spiritum mediam, terreni ponderis et caelestis levitatis admixtione concretam, ex qua monet etiam nos amorem informari et inlabi pectoribus humanis et sensum movere et adfectus fingere et ardorem cupiditatis infundere.

Isti igitur impuri spiritus, daemones, ut ostensum magis ac philosophis, sub statuis et imaginibus consecratis delitiscunt et adflatu suo auctoritatem quasi praesentis numinis consequuntur dum inspirant interim vatibus, dum fanis inmorantur, dum nonnumquam extorum fibras animant, avium volatus gubernant, sortes regunt, oracula efficiunt, falsis pluribus involuta. nam et falluntur et fallunt, ut et nescientes sinceram veritatem et quam sciunt, in perditionem sui non confitentes. sic a caelo deorsum gravant et a deo vero ad materias avocant, vitam turbant, somnos inquietant, inrepentes etiam corporibus occulte, ut spiritus tenues, morbos fingunt, terrent mentes, membra distorquent, ut ad cultum sui cogant, ut nidore altarium vel hostiis pecudum saginati, remissis quae constrinxerant, curasse videantur. hinc sunt et furentes, quos in publicum videtis excurrere, vates et ipsi absque templo, sic insaniunt, sic bacchantur, sic rotantur: par et in illis instigatio daemonis, sed argumentum dispar furoris. (*Oct.* 26.8–27.3)

Just as here Lactantius owed his knowledge of Plato's *Symposium* to Minucius, so he owed a much quoted sentence of the *Timaeus* to *Octavius* 19.14 (p. 79).

Apart from these obvious examples, the claims of Brandt and Beaujeu become much harder to substantiate. It is true that only Lactantius (1.17.6) and Minucius (22.1) make Osiris Isis' *son* (p. 10) but the passages are not altogether similar since Lactantius adds as other examples of the misfortunes of the gods not only Ceres and Proserpina and Cybele, which are in Minucius, but Latona who is not, and the theme, as Beaujeu illustrates, is a commonplace one. So too the immoralities of the gods in *D.I.* 1.10.3–5 look like those in Minucius 23.3–7, but Lactantius adds Castor and Pollux (including a line from a verse translation of Homer: p. 21), Mercury and Liber. Here too we have a τόπος.[9] And there are other such commonplaces where there is not even any linguistic similarity to encourage a belief in direct dependence, e.g. on the antiquity of religious beliefs (20.2 = 2.6.7), the providence of the Universe (17.4 = 1.2.5), *status rectus* (17.2 = 1.5.2 etc.), return from the dead (11.8 = 7.22.10: note that Lactantius does not mention Protesilaus), the anonymity of God (18.10 = 1.6.5), the evils of the games (see p. 89) or the angels as God's companions (26.11 = 1.7.4). Even verbal similarities may not be conclusive. God as the *speculator omnium* (32.9 = 6.18.12) is also in Tertullian, *Apol.* 45.7, and 'deo una domus est mundus hic totus' (33.1 = 4.29.8) was a Stoic aphorism, found in Cicero, *De Rep.* 3.14. Socrates' sobriquet *scurra* (38.5 = 3.20.15) also comes from Cicero (*N.D.* 1.93). There are a few passages where the verbal resemblances are striking (e.g. 3.1 = 2.3.3 'in lapides impingere'; 30.2 = 5.9.15 'pueros aut strangulent aut . . . exponant'; 13.1 = 3.20.10 'quod supra nos, nihil ad nos', elsewhere only quoted by Tertullian (*Ad Nat.* 2.15) and wrongly attributed to Epicurus), but the opening of Book 4 should not be aligned with the opening of the *Octavius* except in the most general sense that this is a traditional form of preface, since Lactantius must have written *consideranti* (BR) not *cogitanti*. Still less should one rely on the similarity between two authors in their lists of *exempla* (p. 43) or catalogue of philosophers (p. 75).

So, although he used the *Octavius*, many of the similarities are due to his use of a handbook of apologetic themes—a natural corollary of his use of an anthology of scriptural quotations.

[9] See M. Pellegrino's note ad loc. in his edition (Turin, 1947).

# XI.  The Bible

LACTANTIUS' primary concern was to propagate the Gospel and
to preach Christ in terms which would convince the educated
pagan. To such a person Oracles, Sibylline or Apolline, or
Hermetic writings or the philosophies of Plato, Cicero, and
Seneca would be more immediately relevant than the crude and
unsophisticated writings of the Old and New Testaments. The
Jews were a small, and tiresome, minority, whose views were
dogmatic and conspicuously uncosmopolitan. It is no wonder,
then, that Lactantius has far more recourse to Virgil and
Lucretius and the Sibylline Oracles than he does to the text of
the Bible. But it is, for us, a matter of the greatest interest to
know not only how thoroughly Lactantius knew the Bible but
how he knew it and what Latin version or versions he had
read: for he was writing nearly 100 years before Jerome's
critical work on an authoritative translation of the Bible. His
citations of the Bible fall into three distinct categories: first, the
quotations in Book 4, where he is expressly citing scriptural
texts to bear out the prophetic mission of Christ and corro-
borating them by analogous pagan texts; secondly, verbatim
quotations in the *D.I.* and in other works; thirdly, less explicit
paraphrases from the Bible.

Lactantius begins by asserting that all who want to understand the truth must concentrate on understanding what the
prophets have to say and study when the various prophecies
were made. He then proceeds to put forward a number of
propositions and support them with appropriate scriptural and
pagan texts. These propositions include, for instance, that God
created an only Son (chapter 6), that this Son was twice born,
in the Spirit and in the flesh (8), and is the Word of God, that
He came to earth in the form of a man (10), because the Jews
had earlier rejected His will (11), and God, therefore, sent His
only Son to win them over, that the Son was born of a Virgin
(12), that the Son would be killed and would rise again to His
father. Lactantius then elaborates this by showing how it was

prophesied that the saviour would come from the house of David and the root of Jesse (13), and would be a great High Priest (14), and how miracles would attend on His appearance on earth (15). The Saviour was to be despised and rejected and killed, but would be resurrected (16). His message was a new Circumcision of the Heart (17), but for this very reason He was to be subjected, like a lamb to the slaughter, to the ignominy of the Crucifixion (18). A prophecy of the destruction of the Temple and of the resurrection (19) is followed by the bequest of the New Covenant (20) and by the Assumption (21). These central propositions were not new in Lactantius: they were the very core of the Christian Gospel and from early times had been buttressed with suitable texts. It was obviously helpful for the missionary or the preacher to have at hand a selection of apposite passages rather than to have, on every occasion, to comb the Scriptures. We do not know how early such selections were made (there are traces of them in Tertullian) but the earliest surviving one was compiled in Latin by Cyprian about A.D. 248–50. It consists of two parts (three books in all since the first part is made up of two books): On the rejection of the Jews and the vocation of the Gentiles, and, On the mystery of Christ; each part is prefaced by a dedication to a certain Quirinus.[1]

The plan and contents of Cyprian's work have close affinities with *D.I.* 4. Cyprian divides his Testimonia into chapters which have headings such as 'That the first Circumcision of the flesh is nullified and that a second, spiritual circumcision, is promised' (1.8), 'That He is called Sheep and Lamb, since He had to be killed' (2.15), 'That salvation for all lies in the Cross' (2.22), 'That Christ had to be born of the seed of David' (2.2) and so on. And he illustrates these propositions with an extensive collection of scriptural quotations which correspond, in whole or in part, to a quite unfortuitous degree, with Lactantius' passages, as the table below shows. Out of seventy-three passages only twenty are not found in both authors, four of those at the end of Book 4 where Lactantius has moved on to another topic not dealt with by Cyprian (70–3). There is also

---

[1] The definitive text is R. Weber, *S. Cypriani Episcopi Opera* (Corpus Christianorum, Series Latina 3, Pars 1). For a brief account see P. Hinchcliff, *Cyprian of Carthage* (Chapman, 1974), 32 ff.

the close grouping of texts both in Lactantius and in Cyprian (see 4–5, 12–13, 14–15, 22–3, 25–7, 33–7, 47–9, 59–62, 64–7) which points to a common principle of selection, and, as we shall see, there are detailed textual similarities in a number of the quotations which point to some mutual interdependence. Now Cyprian was an author whom Lactantius knew, respected and exploited. Of that there is no doubt. He is one of the few to be distinguished individually (5.4.3): 'non defugi laborem ut inplerem materiam quam Cyprianus non est exsecutus in ea oratione qua Demetrianum sicut ipse ait oblatrantem atque obstrepentem veritati redarguere conatur. qua materia non est usus ut debuit: non enim scripturae testimoniis . . . sed argumentis . . . fuerat refellendus.' It was, therefore, natural for Brandt to assume that Lactantius had borrowed all the scriptural material in Book 4 from Cyprian and to attempt to explain away any textual divergences.[2]

But these divergences are very considerable. It is true that our task is not helped in that there appears to be no consistent archetype of Cyprian's *Ad Quirinum*, that there was no uniform text of the old Latin Bible[3] and that the manuscripts of the *D.I.* themselves present successive modifications of what Lactantius wrote. As far as Lactantius' text is concerned, although there are changes from book to book, there is the basic cleavage between those manuscripts (principally R) which have the Constantinian addresses and gnostic additions and those (principally B) which do not (see p. 2). Where BR agree they are the closest recoverable stage to what Lactantius wrote and where B and R differ, R is likely to be the result of a later correction by Lactantius, so that it is impossible to establish a single archetype, let alone a single text of the *D.I.*

I give first of all a numbered list of all the biblical and apocryphal quotations in Book 4 with the corresponding passages in Cyprian.

| No. 1 Lact. | *D.I.*4.6.6. | Cypr. *Ad Quir.* 2.1 | Prov. 8.22–31 |
|---|---|---|---|
| 2 | 4.8.1 | 1.21 | Jer. 1.5 |
| 3 | 4.8.1 | — | Jer. 1.5 |

[2] On Lactantius and the Bible see Pichon, 199 ff.; Monat 1.41–4.

[3] For the pre-Vulgate Latin texts of the Bible see the bibliography in R. Weber, xxxi ff.

| No. | Lact. *D.I.* | Cypr. *Ad Quir.* | |
|---|---|---|---|
| 4 | 4.8.14 | 2.3 | Ps. 33.6 |
| 5 | 4.8.15 | 2.3 | Ps. 44.2 |
| 6 | 4.8.15 | 2.1 | Sir. 24.3–4 |
| 7 | 4.8.16 | 2.3 | John 1.1–3 |
| 8 | 4.11.4 | 1.2 | Jer. 25.4–6 |
| 9 | 4.11.5 | 1.3 | Neh. 9.26 (2 Esdras) |
| 10 | 4.11.6 | 1.2 | 3 Kings (1 Kings) 19.10 |
| 11 | 4.11.8 | 1.16 | Malach. 1.10–11 |
| 12 | 4.11.9 | 1.21 | Ps. 18.44 |
| 13 | 4.11.10 | 1.21 | Isa. 66.18–19 |
| 14 | 4.11.12 | 1.3 | Isa. 1.2–3 |
| 15 | 4.11.13 | 1.3 | Jer. 8.7–9 |
| 16 | 4.12.3 | — | Solomon, Ode 19 |
| 17 | 4.12.4 | 2.9 | Isa. 7.14 |
| 18 | 4.12.7 | — | Ps. 85.12 |
| 19 | 4.12.8 | — | Isa. 63. 10–11 |
| 20 | 4.12.9 | — | Isa. 45.8 |
| 21 | 4.12.10 | 2.21 | Isa. 9.6 |
| 22 | 4.12.12–16 | 2.26 | Dan. 7.13–14 |
| 23 | 4.12.17 | 2.26 | Ps. 110.1 |
| 24 | 4.12.18 | 1.21 | Isa. 45.1–3 |
| 25 | 4.13.7 | 2.6 | Isa. 45.14–16 |
| 26 | 4.13.8 | 2.6 | Baruch 3.36–38 |
| 27 | 4.13.9 | 2.6 | Ps. 45.7–8 |
| 28 | 4.13.10 | 2.10 | Jer. 17.9 |
| 29 | 4.13.10 | — | Isa. 19.20 |
| 30 | 4.13.10 | 2.10 | Num. 24.17 |
| 31 | 4.13.18 | 1.3 | Ps. 28.4–5 |
| 32 | 4.13.19 | 1.21 | Isa. 11.10 |
| 33 | 4.13.20 | 2.11 | Isa. 11.1–3 |
| 34 | 4.13.22 | 2.11 | 2 Sam. 7.4–16 |
| 35 | 4.13.27 | — | Ps. 127.1–2 |
| 36 | 4.14.4 | 1.17 | Ps. 110.3–4 |
| 37 | 4.14.5 | 1.17 | 1 Sam. 2.35 |
| 38 | 4.14.6–9 | 2.13 | Zach. 3.1–8 |
| 39 | 4.15.3 | — | Luke 3.22, Ps. 2.7 |
| 40 | 4.15.13 | 2.7 | Isa. 35.3–6 |
| 41 | 4.16.6 | — | Psa. 1.1 |
| 42 | 4.16.7–10 | 2.14 | Wisd. 2.12–22 |
| 43 | 4.16.14 | — | Ps. 72.6–7 |

| No. 44 | Lact. *D.I.*4.16.15–17 | Cypr. *Ad Quir.* 2.13 | Isa. 53.1–6 |
|---|---|---|---|
| 45 | 4.17.3 | 1.10 | Mic. 4.2–3 |
| 46 | 4.17.6 | 1.18 | Deut. 18.17–18 |
| 47 | 4.17.8 | 1.8 | Jer. 4.3–4 |
| 48 | 4.17.9 | 1.8 | Deut. 30.6 |
| 49 | 4.17.9 | 1.8 | Jos. 5.2 |
| 50 | 4.18.4 | — | Mark 14.58, John 2.19 |
| 51 | 4.18.13 | 2.13 | Isa. 50.5–6 |
| 52 | 4.18.14 | — | Ps. 35.15–16 |
| 53 | 4.18.16 | 2.15 | Isa. 53.7 |
| 54 | 4.18.18 | — | Ps. 69.22 |
| 55 | 4.18.22 | — | 'Esdras' |
| 56 | 4.18.24–25 | 2.15 | Isa. 58, 8–9, 12 |
| 57 | 4.18.26 | — | Ps. 94.21–22 |
| 58 | 4.18.27 | 2.15 | Jer. 11.18–19 |
| 59 | 4.18.29 | 2.22 | Deut. 28.66 |
| 60 | 4.18.29 | 2.22 | Num. 23.19 |
| 61 | 4.18.29 | 2.22 | Zach. 12.10 |
| 62 | 4.18.30 | 2.22 | Ps. 22.17–19 |
| 63 | 4.18.32 | — | 3 Kings (1 Kings) 9.6–9 |
| 64 | 4.19.3 | 2.23 | Amos 8.9–10 |
| 65 | 4.19.4 | 2.23 | Jer. 15.9 |
| 66 | 4.19.8 | 2.24 | Ps. 16.10 |
| 67 | 4.19.8 | 2.24 | Ps. 3.6 |
| 68 | 4.19.9 | 2.25 | Hos. 13.13–14, 6.2 |
| 69 | 4.20.6 | 1.11 | Jer. 31.31–32 |
| 70 | 4.20.7 | — | Jer. 12.7–8 |
| 71 | 4.20.12 | — | Isa. 42.6–7 |
| 72 | 4.21.2–4 | — | Praedicatio Petri |
| 73 | 4.29.10 | — | Isa. 45.14, 44.6 |

A detailed examination of the seventy-three scriptural citations in Book 4 in comparison with Cyprian makes it clear that Lactantius cannot have drawn his material from the *Ad Quirinum* in its present state.[4] This is proved not merely by the

---

[4] There is, however, a further complication. The scribe of MS. H of Lactantius or its ancestors has regularly revised the Biblical text in the light of the Vulgate or a near-Vulgate text, supplying gaps and changing words. The evidence of H, therefore, although interesting in itself, must be ignored for the purpose of establishing what Lactantius wrote.

| 11 | indicat RB | adnuntiat H |
|---|---|---|
| 14 | genui RB | generavi H Cyprian |
| | cognovit RB | agnovit H Cyprian |

twenty passages not to be found in Cyprian but by various omissions by Cyprian in the passages which are common to both authors and, above all, by significant differences of language. Phrases and passages in Cyprian which are not in Lactantius are not significant evidence since they could have been omitted either deliberately by Lactantius, for reasons of clarity or brevity, or accidentally by scribes.

Omissions: 24, 68, 69.

| Language: | LACTANTIUS | CYPRIAN |
|---|---|---|
| 4 | verbo | sermone |
| 11 | clarificabitur | clarificatum est |
| 14 | genui | generavi |
| | cognovit | agnovit |
| | spreverunt | reprobaverunt |
| | percipe auribus | praebe aures |
| 21 | magni consilii | magnae cogitationis |
| 22 | (see p. 102 n. 5) | |
| 24 | obaudire | ut exaudiant |
| 28 | cognovit | cognoscet |
| 32 | principari | imperare |
| | in honore | honor |
| 33 | exiet | exibit |
| 34 | Dominus Deus omnipotens | Dominus |
| | in nomine meo | nomini meo |
| | filio | filium |
| 36 | paenitebit | paenitebitur |
| | genui | generavi |
| | conspectu meo | conspectu Christorum meorum |

| 15 | falsi RB | falsa H Cyprian mendax Vulg. |
|---|---|---|
| 25 | confessione(m) RB | confusionem H Cyprian Vulg. |
| 27 | iniquitatem RB | iniustitiam H Cyprian |
| 35 | in vanum RB | sine causa H |
| 36 | Deus RB | Dominus H Cyprian (LXX) |
| 42 | stultitia RB | malitia H Cyprian |
| | ipsorum RB Cyprian | illorum H |

H supplies the portions of verses 12 and 21 missing in RB
sacramenta RB Cyprian mysteria H Vulg.

| 47 | viri RB | viris H Cyprian |
|---|---|---|
| 49 | sede et RB | sedens H (cf. LXX καθίσας) |
| 54 | potum mihi dederunt acetum RB | potaverunt me aceto H Vulg. |
| 57 | animam RB | in animam H (cf. LXX) |
| 61 | quem RB | in quem H Cyprian |

| Language: LACTANTIUS | | CYPRIAN |
|---|---|---|
| 42 | tormentis | tormento |
| | et sciamus | ut sciamus |
| 45 | deliget | deteget |
| 46 | in os | in ore |
| | tondentibus | tondente |
| 53 | ad immolandum | ad victimam |
| 64 | cantica | omnia cantica |
| 71 | ex vinculis alligatos | a vinculis vinctos |
| | confirmabo | confortabo |

22 is a special case, because there are at this point two texts of the LXX. Lactantius and Cyprian disagree widely between themselves, and give their allegiance to the different branches of the LXX.[5]

These examples must prove that Lactantius did not derive his scriptural material directly from Cyprian (at least from Cyprian's *Ad Quirinum* as we know it). Yet there are further points, which emerge from a comparison of the two authors, that suggest there must be some relationship between the two.

13 Lactantius and Cyprian both omit the geographical details about Tarsis etc.

56 Both omit verses 10 and 11;
'neque insidias ore suo (locutus est Lact.)' Lact. and Cyprian as opposed to LXX οὐδὲ εὑρέθη δόλος ἐν τῷ στόματι αὐτοῦ.

65 Lactantius and Cyprian both omit 'septem'.

37 Both omit τὰ ἐν τῇ ψύχῃ μου.

42 Both omit the ends of verses 12 and 21.

26 Both falsely attribute the passage to Jeremiah.

Given Lactantius' concern for the purity of Latin style, one might hope that he had set out to improve on the coarse and

---

[5] Cyprian tends to agree with the main tradition of LXX, Lactantius with the Theodotion tradition:

καὶ αὐτῷ ἐδόθη ἡ ἀρχὴ καὶ ἡ τιμὴ καὶ ἡ βασιλεία Theod. ~ 'et datum est ei regnum et honor et imperium' Lact.
καὶ ἐδόθη αὐτῷ ἐξουσία LXX ~ 'et data est ei potestas regia' Cyprian.

I am not sure how far one can, or should, use this evidence. Theodotion, known to Irenaeus and used by Origen, came from Pontus or Ephesus, which suggests that his version of the LXX was circulating in the East, while Cyprian knew a Western version. But the fact that he was a Gnostic who lapsed into Judaism may be more relevant for appreciating the general tendency of the anthology of scriptural quotations which Lactantius used.

colloquial Latinity of the Bible that was current in Cyprian's day (cf. e.g. 71 *confirmabo* Lact.: *confortabo* Cyprian). But this is not the explanation of the discrepancies between him and Cyprian. To take two instances:

    32 'principari' is less classical than 'imperare';
    33 'exiet' is less classical than 'exibit'.

Another explanation must be found, and I doubt whether the changes between the first (B) and the second (R) editions of the *D.I.* will provide any help towards discovering it. Yet these changes are substantial and, on the whole, point in the direction of an increasingly accepted text, at least of the Old Testament. A few of the most important are listed below, simply to give some indication of how major the revision must have been.

|   | B | R |
|---|---|---|
| 1 | Dominus | Deus |
|   | fontes | montes |
| 3 | item alibi | item apud eundem |
| 4 | firmati | solidati |
| 7 | illum . . . illo | ipsum . . . ipso (Cyprian) |
| 8 | adfectationibus (Cyprian) | adfectionibus |
| 17 | in utero accipiet (Cyprian) | accipiet in uterum |
| 24 | aperiam tibi (LXX) | om. |
|   | Dominus Deus tuus | om. |
|   | Deus Israel | om. |
| 25 | non nesciebamus | non sciebamus (Cyprian) |
| 27 | Deus Deus (LXX) | Dominus Deus (Cyprian) |
|   | oleum | oleo (Cyprian) |
|   | odisti Vulg. | odio habuisti (Cyprian) |
| 29 | iudicans et sanabit | iudicans sanabit |
| 32 | principari in nationibus | principari in nationes |
| 34 | erit mihi | mihi erit |
| 37 | faciet (Cyprian) | faciat |
| 38 | talarem | poderem (Cyprian, LXX) |
| 40 | pusillo animo | pusilli animi |
| 42 | Dei se (Cyprian) | se Dei |
|   | patrem Deum (Cyprian) | patrem Dominum |
|   | eventura (Cyprian) | ventura |
| 47 | et qui (Cyprian) | qui |
| 53 | tondentibus | tondentibus se |
| 56 | peccata (Cyprian) | peccatum |

|    | B                       | R                                |
|----|-------------------------|----------------------------------|
| 58 | ego autem               | ego                              |
|    | sine macula             | sine malitia (Cyprian, LXX)      |
| 64 | obtenebratur            | obtenebricabitur (Cyprian)       |
| 65 | confusa (Cyprian)       | contusa (LXX)                    |
| 66 | relinquens              | derelinquens (Cyprian)           |
|    | apud                    | ad (Cyprian)                     |
|    | corruptionem (Vulg.)    | interitum (Cyprian)              |
| 67 | somnium                 | somnum                           |
| 68 | nos (Cyprian)           | me                               |
| 69 | neglexi                 | neglexit                         |

Some further light may be shed by the character of some of the quotations.

39 This is a conflation of Luke 3:22 (on Christ's baptism), which in the Vulgate appears as 'tu es filius meus dilectus, in te complacui mihi' (so also the LXX), and Psalm 2:7 υἱός μου εἶ σύ, ἐγὼ σήμερον γεγέννηκά σε. But some of the early Latin versions replaced the Luke text with the text from the Psalms, in order to stress the spiritual rebirth attendant on Baptism and to explain the Holy Spirit in terms of sanctification rather than as the Third Person of the Trinity. This alteration is found in the codices a, b, c, d, ff, l, r of the Vetus Latina and in the Greek Codex Bezae. It is also, significantly, found in Justin, *Dial.* 88, 103, and in certain Valentinian passages in Irenaeus, *Adv. Haer.* 3.10.4, 3.11.2. In other words it was a particularly Gnostic interpretation of scripture, which, no doubt, accounts for Lactantius' use, and is, perhaps, confirmed by the unique description of the dove which descended as 'candida'. That fact is not recorded in any other text but must come from a special Christian tradition. Since, however, Cyprian does not quote this text, it is only of limited value.[6]

7 points in the same direction. The opening words of John were so well known as hardly to admit of any variation. Yet there are two striking differences between Lactantius and Cyprian. The first is the variation between *verbum* and *sermo* (see below). The second concerns the punctuation of the final clause. Lactantius closes the sentence with the words 'factum est nihil' (*nihil est factum* R), omitting the words 'quod factum

---

[6] V. Loi, *Lattanzio*, 114 n. 57. But note Cic. *De Rep.* 2.45 on white as the appropriate colour for gods.

est'. This punctuation occurs also in Novatian, *Trin.* 13 and must be deliberate. It is again a Gnostic interpretation, designed to support their view of creation.

7, however, also shares with 4 one very important feature—the translation of λόγος by *verbum* rather than *sermo* as it figures in Cyprian. That *verbum* was the word which Lactantius had in front of him rather than *sermo* which Cyprian read and which Brandt preferred, is clear from 4.9.1 'sed melius Graeci λόγον· dicunt quam nos verbum sive sermonem'. As *sive* shows (cf. 1.11 16, 7.23), *sermo* is here a new and preferred term and, therefore, cannot have been in the scriptural text, which Lactantius used. *Sermo* was the translation of the Greek favoured by African tradition of the Vetus Latina[7] and even by Tertullian. It was predictably the translation mainly used by Cyprian in his voluminous writings. *Verbum* was the European term and it may be significant that it is the term used by Novatian predominantly, including citations of this specific text.[8] In other words, the substitution of *verbum* for *sermo* indicates a collection of Testimonia that was known in Western Europe as opposed to Africa. I doubt if there was any theological importance in the change (the Gnostics do not appear to have given particular interpretations to either word), but it is at first sight surprising that Lactantius, himself an African, should prefer a non-African to an African text.

There are a number of passages cited by Lactantius which do not occur at all in Cyprian. It is striking that the majority of them occur in particular chapters (e.g. 16, 18, 19, 20 in chapter 12; 50, 52, 54, 55, 57 in chapter 18; 70, 71 in chapter 20) and that these chapters have no corresponding headings in Cyprian. Chapter 20 is devoted to the enlightenment brought by Christ. The overtones of the argument, especially the concluding sentence, are strongly Gnostic and the same exegesis is found quite independently in Eusebius, *Ecl. Proph.* 202. So close indeed is the resemblance that it confirms Volkmann's reading of *mali* for the manuscript *malis* (4.20.13; cf. σειραῖς τῶν ἰδίων ἁμαρτίων). Chapter 12, as Wlosok has argued,[9] is also a self-

[7] F. C. Burkitt, *The Old Latin and the Itala*, 13; H. F. van Soden, *Das Neue Testament in Afrika*, 71; V. Loi, *Lattanzio*, 210–11.

[8] C. Mohrmann, *Vig. Chris.* 3 (1949), 167 n. 11.

[9] *Studia Patristica* 4 (1961), 234 ff.

contained entity. The arguments for Christ's birth from a virgin
centre on the interpretation of Solomon, Ode 19. This apocryphal ode did not stand in the African canon of the Bible (cf.
*verbum/sermo* above) but the odes in general were quarried by
the author of the late-third-century Gnostic work, *Pistis Sophia*,
and Ode 19, in particular, was used by Eusebius, *Dem. Evang.*
10.499 c–d in a christological argument of a markedly anti-
Jewish kind. The existence of some work, Gnostic and anti-
Jewish, which contained a number of non-canonical *testimonia*
is confirmed by other evidence.[10] 3 ('beatus qui erat antequam
nasceretur') is a strange text which does not occur in the Bible
but is found in Irenaeus, *Epid.* 43 and in *Evang. Thom.*, Logion
19. The exposition of Zacharias 3.1–8 (no. 38) is closely paralleled by Eusebius, *Ecl. Proph.* 123.23 ff. (cf. μηδαμῶς ἐκεῖνα τῷ
λεγομένῳ ἁρμόνει ~ 'in quos nihil congruit') but Eusebius, it
should be repeated, had no knowledge of Lactantius. The
clearest proof comes from 55 which is elsewhere only quoted by
Justin (*Dial.* 72.1) who says it was suppressed by the Jews from
their texts of the Bible. In fact the use of the word πάσχα makes
it much more probable that it was invented by the Christians
for controversial purposes. The character of that controversy can
be seen from 4.7.1 (see p. 22) where Lactantius discusses the
etymology of χριστός and comments on the false use of
ἠλειμμένος as a translation. It is relevant that ἠλειμμένος is
found as the translation in Aquila, the Jewish anti-Christian
translation of the Bible.

Lactantius promised a separate work *Contra Iudaeos* (7.1.26),
to supplement Tertullian and Cyprian. We do not know
whether he ever actually undertook it, but the passages which
we have examined belong to that tradition. Certain conclusions
follow. The most likely place to find these apocryphal traditions
was in the Greek East and, therefore, Book 4 was composed, or
planned, during his time at Nicomedia.[11] (Whether his conversion occurred here or, as Stevenson and others hold, in
Africa is not immediately clear.) These passages have been
added to a basic framework which was either a revised or a

---

[10] Note also the substitution of *stultitia* (Gnostic) for the canonical *malitia* in
4.16.10.

[11] V. Loi, *Mélanges Mohrmann*, 61–74 argued from the date given for the Crucifixion that Book 4 was composed in Gaul.

careless edition of Cyprian's *Testimonia*. The addition is likely
to have been made by Lactantius himself.

The final proof of this, if proof be still needed, lies in the last
quotation in this long section of prophetic and biblical testimony. The destruction of the Jews is foretold by Peter and Paul
(1.21.2–4). This *Praedicatio*, as Lactantius calls it, is one of the
well-known non-canonical books of the early Church.[12] It is
usually called the Praedicatio Petri or Κήρυγμα Πέτρου and
was available as early as the mid-second century when Aristides
read it. Origen and Clement of Alexandria were among the
Fathers who used its material most extensively, but its tendency
is clear from the fact that Heracleon, a Gnostic at Rome in the
mid-third century, availed himself of it (Origen, *Comm. in Ioann.*),
and from the quotations which show that it was directed against
the Jews. It claimed, among other things, that the Apostles had
offered the Jews twelve years in which to repent and that the
Jews worshipped angels, just as the Greeks worshipped idols,
whereas the true knowledge of God was disclosed to Christians.
Harnack, who compiled the great collection of early Christian
writing, unwarrantably rejected this quotation of Lactantius,
but it fits with all we know of the *Praedicatio* and with all the
tendencies we have recognized in the non-Cyprianic quotations
of the Bible.

Verbatim quotations of the Bible are rare in the other books
of the *D.I.* and non-existent in the other works, except the
*Epitome*. This is consistent with Lactantius' expressed purpose
not to introduce evidence which might be *a priori* unacceptable
(4.5.3 '(prophetarum) nunc uti necesse est: quod in prioribus
libris ne facerem temperavi'). There are in fact only seven,
two from the Psalms (7.14.9 = Ps. 90.4; 7.20.5 = Ps. 1.5) and
the rest from the New Testament. The noticeable feature which
they share in common is that they are very free quotations,
suggesting memory rather than research. Thus Matth. 5.32 is
quoted in indirect speech (6.23.33), as is Ephes. 4.26 (6.18.33
'praecipit deus non occidere solem super iram nostram'), and

---

[12] A. Harnack, *Geschichte der altchristlichen Literatur bis Eusebius* (Leipzig, 1893),
1.25 ff. (no. 21); P. Carrington, *The Early Christian Church* (Cambridge, 1957),
2.8–10. M. Hornschuh (in E. Hennecke–W. Schneemelcher, *Neutestamentliche
Apokryphen* (Tübingen, 1964 ii, p. 57)), is also sceptical, doubting the identification
of Lactantius' work with the *Praedicatio Petri* and concluding that no inferences
can be made about it.

Psalm 1.5 = Luke 18.14 is quoted with *extollit* for *exaltat* (5.15.9: see Monat ad loc.)—not a textual variant. Similarly careless is 'tamquam unus dies' in Psalm 90.4 for ὡς ἡ ἡμέρα ἡ ἐχθὲς ἥτις διῆλθεν. 6.12.41, however ('si audieris, inquit (Deus), preces supplicis tui, et ego audiam tuas: si misertus laborantium fueris, et ego in tuo labore miserebor. si autem non respexeris nec adiuveris, et ego animum tuum contra te geram tuisque te legibus iudicabo'), bears only the slightest resemblance to Luke 6.36 and may come from an apocryphal Gospel, if it is not a loose elaboration by Lactantius himself. Brandt was unable to place 6.23.38 ('si quis hoc, inquit, facere potuerit, habebit eximiam incomparabilemque mercedem'). He compared 1 Cor. 7.7 or Matth. 19.12 but Matth. 5.12 is much closer, although still very far from a literal or exact quotation.

Lactantius does not seem to have had a special reason for using the quotations that he does: they occur apparently at random, without any logical selection. Yet it would be wrong to infer that his acquaintance with the Scriptures was, therefore, sketchy. His knowledge is wider and more pervasive than that.

# XII.   Conclusion

THE library resources of Carthage or Alexandria or Rome were boundless but Lactantius was a traveller and could not rely on finding what he needed at Nicomedia or Trier. Nor, as we have seen, was he a scholar of great range and acumen: indeed his familiarity with Greek literature is slight, which may partly account for his evident unhappiness in Bithynia. The preceding chapters have attempted to discover what works he either used in writing *D.I.* or knew sufficiently well to be able to quote from memory.

The resulting list is an interesting one. No Greek classical prose or poetry. His Greek reading is confined to oracular literature—Sibylline Oracles, oracles of Apollo and Hystaspes, some Orphic poems and some hermetic works—most of which may have been known to him through a single compilation or Theosophy. His Latin reading of poetry extends to Lucretius, Horace, Virgil, Ovid's *Fasti* and *Metamorphoses*, and Persius, *Satires* 2 and 6: for the rest he is indebted to one or more *florilegia*. Of classical prose authors Cicero leads the field, although the absence of so many speeches and other works, such as the *De Finibus* and the letters, is striking. He knew Livy's first Decade and Sallust's *Catiline* but not Tacitus nor, probably, Varro. He knew Seneca's philosophical works and an edition of Book 1 of Valerius Maximus. Aulus Gellius he came across after writing the *D.I.*, but he may have had access to a similar compendium for some of his antiquarian and mythological material, unless it was all to be found in a commentary on the *Aratea*. An anthology provided him with most of his biblical and apocryphal quotations and, probably, with those apologetic commonplaces which he could not locate in Minucius, Cyprian, Theophilus, or Tertullian's *Apologeticum*.

In his reading he offers an interesting comparison with Tertullian a hundred years before him, and Augustine or Jerome seventy years later. Tertullian was writing during the great archaizing revival of the late second century, when old books were unearthed and reread, and before the political breakdown of the third century. He still knew Herodotus, Plato, Josephus, Pliny the younger, Tacitus, Juvenal, Ennius, Varro, perhaps the elder Cato—to name but a few.[1]

In the late fourth century, pagans and Christians re-discovered some forgotten classics, especially Juvenal and Tacitus, but in the intervening period much literature has been lost beyond recall. Thus Jerome was familiar not only with the range of works which Lactantius knew but also with Plautus, Lucan, and Martial.[2] But in other respects he and Augustine are very similar to Lactantius. Augustine knew little Greek and derived his Platonic philosophy from Cicero (*Epist.* 118.2.10), whereas Jerome did not become closely acquainted with Greek literature until thirty years after his school days. On the other hand Virgil and Cicero's works, above all the *Hortensius*, meant much to Augustine (*C.D.* 1.3; *Conf.* 3.4.7).[3] The same picture emerges from a study of Ausonius,[4] or of Claudian[5] although his interest and opportunities gave him a slightly wider range.

Lactantius, therefore, in a real sense marks the beginning of the Middle Ages. Between the time of Tertullian and his own day the great process of survival had already jettisoned many literary treasures of Athens and Rome to oblivion.

---

[1] T. D. Barnes, *Tertullian*, 196 ff.

[2] J. N. D. Kelly, *Jerome* (London, 1975), 10–17.

[3] Peter Brown, *Augustine of Hippo* (London, 1967), 36–7. A friend of Augustine's knew all Virgil and much Cicero by heart (*De Anim. et eius Orig.* 4.7.9).

[4] R. P. H. Green, *C.Q.* 27 (1977), p. 441 ff.

[5] Alan Cameron, *Claudian* (Oxford, 1970), 305 ff.

# Index Locorum

1

## 2